PRAISE FOR OVE

"Kay Sprinkel Grace is synonymous with clear thinking and sound wisdom. In this authoritative, no-nonsense book she combines impressive experience and insights with wit and polished writing to produce a treasure-house of ideas for her readers. A 'must have' for all serious fundraisers."
Ken Burnett,
Author, *Relationship Fundraising*

"Offering a wealth of insight, *Over Goal!* is a revitalizing look at our field from a seasoned and always positive pro."
Sarah Harrison, Vice President, Advancement
The Denver Foundation

"In pages rich with practical advice, Kay Sprinkel Grace's wisdom, experience, and willingness to think outside the box come shining through. *Over Goal!* will recharge the batteries of dedicated nonprofit leaders everywhere."
Mike Cortés,
Director, Institute for Nonprofit Organization Management
University of San Francisco

"*Over Goal!* is a handy guide for meeting today's challenges in nonprofit fundraising. Kay Sprinkel Grace's is a voice of accumulated experience and wisdom, relevant and up to date, coaching you to sustained success in fundraising."
Timothy Seiler, Director, The Fund Raising School
The Center on Philanthropy at Indiana University

"Reading *Over Goal!* is like enjoying a series of leisurely lunches with a brilliant, wise, and down to earth fundraiser. Almost invisibly, Kay Sprinkel Grace transfers a philosophy and sense of fundraising."
Jan Masaoka, President and CEO
Compasspoint Nonprofit Services

"*Over Goal!* is a must read."
Lee C. Palmer Everding, Chair
Communicom

"*Over Goal!*" is a refreshingly straightforward book, sure to inspire and focus your fundraising efforts."
Nancy L. Wells, Associate Vice President for Development
Stanford University Arrillaga Alumni Center

"Well known for her insight o: ent,
Kay Sprinkel Grace shares that ins
practical advice for managing a fun
Paulette Maehara, Presiden
Association of Fundraising

Also by Kay Sprinkel Grace

*High Impact Philanthropy: How Donors,
Boards, and Nonprofit Organizations
Can Transform Communities*
2000
Co-author with Alan Wendroff
(ISBN 0-471-36918-7)

*Beyond Fund Raising: New Strategies for
Nonprofit Innovation and Investment*
1997
(ISBN 0471-16232-9)

OVER GOAL!

What You Must Know to Excel at Fundraising Today

KAY SPRINKEL GRACE

Emerson
& Church
PUBLISHERS

First printed March 2003

10 9 8 7 6 5 4 3 2 1

Printed in the United States of America

This text is printed on acid-free paper.

Copies of this book are available from the
publisher at discount when purchased in
quantity for boards of directors or staff.

Emerson & Church, Publishers
P.O. Box 338 • Medfield, MA 02052
Tel. 508-359-0019 • Fax 508-359-2703

Library of Congress Cataloging-in-Publication Data

Grace, Kay Sprinkel.
  Over goal! : what you must know to excel at fundraising today / Kay
Sprinkel Grace.
     p. cm.
Includes index
  ISBN 1-889102-14-8 (pbk: alk paper)
  1. Fund raising. 2. Nonprofit organizations--Finance. I. Title.
HV41.2.G726 2003
361.7'068'1--dc21   2002153018

This book is dedicated to my son, friend and
professional colleague, Greg. His multi-dimensional
and untiring support has given me space, time
and inspiration to reflect and write.

THE AUTHOR

Kay Sprinkel Grace is a prolific writer, creative thinker, inspiring speaker, and reflective practitioner. Her passion for philanthropy and its capacity to transform donors, organizations, and communities is well-known in the U.S. and internationally.

With an increasingly powerful vision for the way in which organizations, funders, and communities must partner to resolve community problems and enhance cultural, educational, and other resources, Kay has increased the understanding and motivation of donors and organizations regarding the importance of the philanthropic sector in today's changing and challenging society.

She lives in San Francisco and is an enthusiastic photographer, traveler, hiker and creative writer. When not writing, speaking, or consulting, you can find her with her children and grandchildren who live in San Francisco, upstate New York, and France.

TABLE OF CONTENTS

Introduction

PART ONE: FUNDRAISING

1	Successful Nonprofit Organizations	13
2	Positioning Your Organization as a Solid Investment	23
3	The Role of Organizational Culture in Fund Raising	29
4	Fundraising Communications	37
5	Creating or Revising a Mission Statement	47
6	Understanding the Motivations of Major Donors	55
7	Keeping Your Prospect Pipeline Full	63
8	Cultivating Your Donors	73
9	Getting Your Board to Make Personal Solicitations	81
10	The Dynamics of a Solicitation Call	91
11	The New Realities of Capital Campaigns	101
12	Recruiting and Retaining a Capital Campaign Committee	109
13	Conducting a Campaign Feasibility Study	117
14	Transformational Gifts	123
15	Planning and Implementing a Year-End Fundraising Program	135
16	Starting a Stewardship Program	143

17 Evaluating Your Fundraising Effectiveness   151

18 Fundraising in a Changing Economy   159

19 Overcoming Your Donors' Psychic Poverty   167

20 Hiring Development Staff   175

21 Hiring a Development or Organizational Consultant   185

PART TWO: BOARD AND ORGANIZATIONAL DEVELOPMENT

22 Recruiting and Enlisting the Best Board Possible   195

23 The Dynamics of Successful Board Meetings   203

24 Recruiting Younger People for Your Board   209

25 Keeping Your Board and Staff Partnership in Balance   217

26 Organizing a Successful Board Retreat   225

27 Collaborating with Other Organizations   235

28 Strategic Institutional Planning   243

    Index   253

INTRODUCTION

It's a new world for nonprofit organizations. The 21st century began with a bang, creating even more demands for responsive, innovative, and effective programs and services.

Communities are looking increasingly at nonprofits to partner with them to address new or continuing needs in education, health, the environment, arts and culture, and the many causes that address other social, human, or quality of life needs.

Government funding, which began eroding in the U.S. and globally in the 1980s, hasn't been restored and, with the dramatically volatile economy, corporate and foundation funding has also become less stable.

While individuals remain the largest source of funding in the U.S., and many are also investing overseas, the overall outlook is one where the need for nonprofit services is exceeding the optimism about how to fund them.

And, the practice of fundraising is changing more rapidly than ever. More sophisticated donors, expecting accountability, transparency, and disclosure, are demanding new performance standards. Competition is stiff, with many organizations vying for the same limited dollars and seemingly addressing the same community needs. Donors are asking for more clarity, collaboration, and evidence of good management.

On the governance side, volunteers seem to be in short supply, and the board members everyone wants to recruit are over-committed.

If these are the realities, what are the best strategies for creating new performance standards for nonprofits? How can we meet donor and client demands, build boards that will have energy and vision, and navigate the rough waters of a new century and a seemingly new economy?

This book was written to address these issues in common sense language. It is drawn from my experience as a development professional and consultant for nearly 25 years, and from an additional 15 years as a volunteer leader.

Practical, provocative, and focused, this book travels quickly but deliberately through many aspects of the challenges we face, offering solutions and ideas well-grounded in experience.

While the primary focus is on fund raising, the book honors the fundamental truth that without good governance, fund raising is nearly impossible. The chapters on governance are as important as the chapters on fund raising. The two functions are inseparable.

Whether you are a seasoned or novice professional, or a veteran or new volunteer, I think you will get a great deal out of this book.

My own view of the future of philanthropy and nonprofits is very optimistic. I feel that America's voluntary sector activities – and the ways in which they have been carried overseas as our most meaningful social export – have never been more poised to have a powerful impact on society.

I invite all of you to learn more about how you can meet and exceed your goals, increase your impact, and stay comfortably ahead of the waves of change.

San Francisco, California   Kay Sprinkel Grace

Part One

◆

FUNDRAISING

1

SUCCESSFUL NONPROFIT ORGANIZATIONS

Donors invest in them. Talented professionals want to work for them. The media cover their activities. The community talks about them. Leaders want to serve on their boards. And you know and admire (and perhaps even envy) them.

They are the successful organizations in your community that attract money, talent, publicity, and leadership while other organizations wonder why.

They can be small, medium or large. They may work in the arts, social services, medical care, environment, or any of the other critical areas served by the public benefit sector. And they need not be venerable to be perceived as valuable: new organizations with an exciting vision and plan and a mission that reflects an unmet community need will attract leaders, funders, and professionals.

So what are the secrets?

Here's what you should know about the qualities, practices, and attributes of successful nonprofit organizations.

Unwavering vision.

Through good times and bad, up cycles and downturns, stability and change, the vision of their leadership – and their commitment to working towards that vision – doesn't falter.

One medical center, suffering from the whipsaw of two mergers, financial hemorrhages, changes in leadership, and general resistance to philanthropic support for already-expensive care, is now thriving again.

The center raises between $13 and $15 million each year in annual support and planned gifts while other centers in the same community founder.

What is the difference? Unwavering vision. The board stayed with the organization and continued to advocate for its merits as an investment. The foundation staff, undergoing its own merger and transition, kept its vision strong and its leadership was untiring. The new medical center CEO was a trusted physician who was bold, trustworthy, and built confidence.

It remains the most admired medical center in the community and, among all kinds of organizations, is one of the most distinguished.

Confidence.

Confidence begets confidence.

Organizations that are confident of the integrity of their mission, the quality of their vision, and their ability to deliver programs and services that make a difference are far more attractive to investors than those constantly apologizing for the sector, their lack of resources, or their performance. As a result, investors gain confidence and continue to support the organization.

A very small theater company was determined to take its unique performances overseas. Confident of receiving foundation funding for the trip, the theatre group was disappointed when its request was denied.

But the setback didn't deter the group. They enlisted a friend who knew the funder. She was convinced that the performers and the artistic director had an excellent product and would fulfill the aspirations of the foundation if given the opportunity.

She told the funder he had overlooked a major investment opportunity. He relented, provided the funding and now – years later – is still supporting the company for its annual trips overseas.

That success has attracted other funders and given the company a visibility and reputation that's reflected in increased attendance and support.

No mission drift.

Mission drift, that dangerous condition whereby organizations focus more intently on their own organizational issues than issues in the community, kills success. Passion has to be fanned and fed.

Public passion arises out of admiration for the product and performance of an organization and the connection people feel with its mission. Board members are eventually driven off by organizations in which there's no regular connection with mission, and funders eventually stop investing in groups whose entire message is about their organizational issues and difficulties (including financial shortfalls) rather than the impact they're making in the community.

Public benefit corporations exist for the public benefit: be sure you're looking through your windows into the community, and not just into mirrors, when you do your planning, marketing, fundraising, and recruitment. Talk about the needs you're meeting, not the needs you have.

Clarity of values.

With successful organizations, there's no doubt about what they value. It's woven into their vision, frames their mission, and guides their staff and volunteers.

But it's one thing to speak values and another to evidence them through your programs, outreach, and marketing.

The major success of Sage Hill School in Orange County, a new independent high school, is largely attributable to its comfort with and dedication to integrating its values into every aspect of its operations: recruitment of board, fund raising, recruitment of faculty, admission of students, curriculum, extra curricular activities, disciplinary and other standards.

Marketing and enrollment materials sing with the freshness and clarity of the school's values-based approach to education and community involvement. Banners with words like "commitment," "excellence," "integrity," and others fly from the interior roofline.

As I was visiting the campus one day, a young man came up to me and said how much he liked being a student there. We chatted about his reasons and then, looking up at the banners, he pointed and said, "I got that award last year at school closing." Not seeing which one he meant, I asked which one. "Integrity," he said. I responded by asking him what integrity meant. His reply has lingered with me: "It means being true to others and true to yourself." A good lesson for a 17-year-old and for all of us.

Sage Hill has raised $34 million and is entering into a new funding phase. It has a dedicated board and its founders' vision is enacted every day in every classroom, through service learning in the community, in the boardroom and administrative offices, and on the playing fields.

A sense of abundance.

Successful organizations don't whine. They realize that philanthropy comes from abundance and creates abundance, and they're instrumental in creating a sense of abundance among those who use their services, fund their programs, and give time as volunteers.

An organization that houses and provides job training and child care for working poor and homeless is fast becoming one of the most successful organizations in its community.

Its administrative facilities are modest, its mission difficult, its successes often hard to measure. But the organization realizes that its impact isn't really in numbers, it is in lives.

The group has captured that as their measure of abundance. At their annual dinner – attended by nearly 1,000 people in the community – there was hushed attention paid as a young woman who benefited from the program spoke of her vision for herself and others like her, and told not of what she didn't have but of what she'd been given by this program: hope.

While other programs serving this same population tend to focus on their needs, this program focuses on the needs it is meeting. Their spirit of abundance has been contagious, and the interest of high-profile leaders and donors in the community is growing.

Courage.

A strong attribute of leaders, it also characterizes organizations. Courage to lead and to know when to follow. Courage to take calculated risks if the result will advance the success of their mission. Courage to make tough decisions about people, ideas, and programs.

A much-loved but badly managed organization tried in vain to keep its doors open. Revelations about the true financial condition of the organization began emerging and the executive director (and nearly the entire staff) had to step down.

Community outreach for funding and support rallied for a while, but ultimately it was clear the organization had run its course.

One board member, with extensive corporate experience, stepped forward and led the process of phasing out the organization. Sadness, agony, regrets, and remorse accompanied the courageous determination to close the doors with dignity and honor.

Its demise had been prevented by emergency funding in previous years, but the courage to know that this was the time to "pull the plug" has left the community with good feelings about an organization that now no longer exists.

Other similar organizations stepped forward to embrace its members, and the board can feel good about the process and the results even if it mourns the loss of this resource for the community.

Short of having to muster the courage to close, the courage of successful organizations is most often seen in decisions to take a stand on a particular treatment or service program that's in jeopardy, courage to "de-enlist" board members who no longer have time or interest, to evaluate and dismiss leadership or employees who aren't fulfilling the mission through their work, and the courage to set standards and evaluate performance and programs.

Transparency and regular communication.

Transparency isn't a buzzword, it is a watchword.

Successful organizations remain successful by being transparent about mission, performance, problems, and achievements. They communicate with the board, donors, and the community. Their newsletters don't just feature board members having parties: they tell stories and present statistics about the impact they're having.

The story above about the organization closing its doors is also an excellent example of failure to be transparent. The staff didn't reveal even to the board the true financial picture – if they had, the closing might have been averted. Donors weren't informed of the true situation. Neither were vendors.

Pride often blocks our willingness to be transparent. Organizations that are perceived as successful are those whose numbers and reports are trusted by their board and the public. They're the ones that continually convey their impact in the community, measured against their mission.

As we increasingly view contributions as investments, it's even more necessary to be transparent with our investors. The two bottom lines of the public benefit sector are gauged in return on values and return on investment: not a financial return, but the knowledge that the money is handled well and invested wisely in programs needed in the community.

Our sector has come a great distance in its ability and willingness to measure and report results – we must continue that trend if we are to be successful.

An emphasis on donor development, not just fundraising.

Successful organizations spend time and money on developing relationships, not just on raising money. Donor development is the key function in successful fundraising, and yet too often we say we don't have time or money to cultivate and steward our donors.

One of the lessons we learn from our friends in the corporate sector is that it's easier to re-enlist an existing "customer" than it is to go out and get a new one. We need only to look at the cost of donor acquisition, as opposed to renewal, to know that is true for our sector as well.

Make the case for a budget allocation for cultivation of your prospects and stewardship of your donors. Loyalty of donors – like loyalty of board members – distinguishes successful organizations from those still striving for success.

Focus on donor development, and the money will follow. People will feel good about their engagement with you, and will keep renewing the gift. An emphasis on stewardship is one of the hallmarks of successful organizations.

Continual planning.

I'm always amazed when I receive a call from an organization saying it needs a new plan, that its five-year plan is nearly up. Successful organizations always have a three to five year plan in place. They use the "rolling base" process that requires an annual evaluation of the current year progress and the addition of a new year to the plan.

Then, once every three to five years, they conduct the zero-based process that extensively surveys the organization and the marketplace and they hone their vision and create a new plan.

Those who are successful in business, finance, government, and the other sectors we draw on for leadership increasingly expect that we'll have a sound planning and evaluation process.

Respect, camaraderie and fun.

Successful organizations have respect for each other on the staff level, respect for the board and volunteers, a sense of team commitment, and the time and permission to play.

Ours is serious work, but we don't have to make it a drill. One organization, barely making payroll and budget for a while, would have weekly celebrations (with beer and pizza provided by a board member). Why? Because they made it through another week.

That was 14 years ago, and today the agency is thriving because people there felt like a team, played like a team and celebrated like a team.

One of the most successful children's services agencies in a community can attribute much of its success to the integrated way in which the board and staff work together, to the sense of teamwork on the board, and to the way in which the staff support each other.

One therapist, working tirelessly with an autistic child who had experienced years of frustration as he came close to speech but couldn't cross that threshold, came running out of her office one day shouting, "He talked! He talked!" Next day, her fellow staff members had a T-shirt ready for her which she proudly wore. It said, "Damn I'm Good."

Board members and other volunteers became aware of this, and the accomplishment gave them the idea of having a staff appreciation event. It has become a tradition.

This continues to be an organization that attracts top community leaders and major funders – and it's more than 50 years since it was founded.

•••

If you want to be successful, begin thinking success. Focus on your abundance, not your shortfalls, and focus on the people who make your work possible: those who lead, those who fund, and those you serve. Success breeds success: start now.

2

POSITIONING YOUR ORGANIZATION AS A SOLID INVESTMENT

"If you always do what you've always done, you'll always be what you've always been." Anonymous

While ordinarily applied to the ruts we can get into in our own lives, that little saying applies to nonprofit organizations as well.

If we're to grow to meet the market demand for our services and the increasing expectations of our donors, we have to start doing things differently. And, we need to let our constituencies know we're making changes based on what we see as their needs.

There is an ironic aspect to our organizations that is becoming more obvious as the pace of society quickens. It is this. We are change agents, yet we're extraordinarily slow to change.

Part of this is the result of our governance structure — gaining volunteer board consensus around organizational change requires much more discussion than in a corporate model of governance.

Another contributor to our sometimes lengthy response to change is the lack of resources to implement change. Management-thin, we struggle to divert precious time towards governance or leadership growth and reform, and find that we must more appropriately focus on program delivery or marketing.

All sectors of America's economy are in flux, and the nonprofit sector is no exception. Like our for-profit colleagues, we have been swept up into the technology whirlwind, and the expectations of our clients and investors have accelerated with what often feels like microprocessor speed.

Scrambling to remain competitive in the philanthropic sector, it's becoming urgent that we adjust our systems and structure to be more flexible, more accountable, and more attractive to our investors.

The competition for major gifts grows more complex. Here are the steps for positioning your organization as an attractive, sturdy, vibrant, and accessible investment.

Be open.

The mystique of separateness that surrounded nonprofits in the 1970s, 80s, and even into the 90s has been stripped away. We're now expected to be able partners with the corporate and government sectors in building our communities.

Because we exist in the public trust, we must be open with our vision, finances, governance, results, and problems. Major donors aren't going to make an investment in an organization about which they know too little.

Drawn to the issues we address, and inspired by the passion those issues generate, investors need to know how you're managing their investment, what the impact of that investment has been, and what overall progress your efforts contribute to addressing the issues they are most concerned about.

Be accessible.

People with money but little experience in philanthropy complain that they'd like to give, but organizations don't respond either quickly enough or clearly enough.

A donor concerned about an issue views the nonprofit as a ve-hicle for solving the problem (human or societal) or enhancing the resources (cultural, artistic). If the vehicle doesn't respond, the do-nor will go to another and another until a responsive organization is found.

One donor confided recently that he'd "given up" trying to give money toward a particular issue because he "got the run-around" from every organization he contacted.

Our structure, lack of adequate management, and often-poor systems deter people who are willing investors but unfamiliar with how to access us. Demystify the process. Let people know what you do and how they can help. Keep it simple: a 1-2-3 step guide in your literature or on your website.

Invest in good management - it will pay enormous returns.

Although it's important to keep your staff funding ratio strongly weighted towards those who deliver your program, it's equally im-portant to have a CEO and management team that have expertise, passion, and well-honed management skills.

Plenty of courses exist if your CEO is short on skills but long on integrity and passion — university-based courses or professional classes provide skill-building in leadership, financial management, personnel issues, or vision-setting.

The previously perceived gulf between nonprofit and for-profit management skills sets is now largely ignored: major donors are looking for nonprofit managers with the ability to perform and re-spond like the corporate managers with whom they may be more familiar.

Under-investing in the administrative and financial management of your organization can cost you more than you save ... considering lost gifts, and lost opportunities.

Evaluate how well the management and governance structure is working in your organization.

The way in which nonprofits are governed is based on state laws and is therefore fairly formulaic. A few well known models have been tried, written about, and either kept or rejected. In evaluating the literature on governance, it may be time for the sector as a whole to consider whether the basic governance structure of nonprofits really works in the 21st century.

Executive directors are burning out at a forest fire rate, and development directors are diminishing in number. Even program directors, fueled by the passion of their work, find the board/staff balance a difficult one, and are concerned about keeping it appropriate.

For an investor, these issues can be critical. Within the parameters of your state laws and your own by-laws, take time to evaluate whether there's a better model of governance for your organization, one that will allow it to respond to change and opportunity more readily.

Stay relevant.

Because nonprofits are values and vision driven, they can fall into the trap where their programs (or at least the description of them) can seem to be irrelevant to a changing community. We compound the problem when we also position as "charities" rather than "investments."

If we consider ourselves as charities, we are in danger of developing the feeling that people are obligated to invest in us. Nothing could be further from the truth. You are competing for the investment of discretionary funds — nonprofits are another form of community investment.

On your website, in your printed materials, and on every public occasion, convey why your organization and its programs — venerable and trusted or new and exciting — are highly relevant to the constantly emerging needs of your community.

Keep your mission fresh by framing it with current statistics about the marketplace: for example, how many children need therapy for learning disabilities, how many adolescents have turned to drugs.

Organizations cannot be lulled by their own successes: after all, "if they always do what they've always done...."

When you do change, let it be known.

Slow to change because of our structure and systems, we should be quick to let our community of constituents and investors know when we have changed and what the impact of that change is going to be.

News about planned, responsive, and thoughtful change raises the perception people have of our organizations — we find ourselves described as "cutting edge" and "innovative" rather than stagnant or traditional.

Soon, that public perception can begin to set expectations and even change the way people on the inside view the organization.

Use the best technology you can afford to communicate with the public.

The cost of staying current with new technology drifts downward every day. It's no longer a luxury to have a website or email - it is a necessity. To be accessible, and viewed as an organization in the mainstream (or ahead of the wave), you need to have technology that works.

Moreover, if you're going to invest in a website, invest in a web master. Nothing is more off-putting to a potential donor than visiting your website in September and finding it hasn't been updated since May. Likewise, if you have an email link, be sure you respond.

Letting hundreds of inquiries pile up is foolish. If you are short on funds but long on ambition and ideas, talk with a foundation, corporation, or individual funder about underwriting for the website and about a loaned person to get you started.

Major gifts seldom come in over email, but the seed for major gifts is planted very often by someone who visits your website and makes an inquiry. From that point on, it is up to you.

Make all your internal and external reports for finance and development documents you are proud to share.

Another aspect of technology within organizations is in accounting and reporting. We have passed the stage where errors and lateness are tolerated by staff, board, or funders. Particularly for major donors, accuracy in gift reporting and acknowledgement lays the foundation for good stewardship.

Without this basic attention to good records and good reporting, all the stewardship in the world (events, plaques, notes) won't encourage further involvement.

Be proud and positive that you're part of the most dynamic philanthropic era in history.

We are professionals and volunteers in rare times. Our sector is performing well in chaotic change, and it can perform better. The pay-off for higher performance is more investment from major donors. They are looking for a good place to invest their money so their communities will thrive. Become that place.

•••

In sum, position your organization as a place where vision and goals are well-communicated internally and externally, and where the sense of making a sound investment is keen.

3

THE ROLE OF ORGANIZATIONAL CULTURE IN FUNDRAISING

When Tom Peters and Bob Waterman went in search of excellence more than two decades ago, one of the many things they discovered was the significant role of corporate culture.

Describing it as both the hardest and the softest aspect of organizations, they cited its role in determining the behavior, performance, and perception of an organization and its employees.

In characterizing their observations, they drew on the work of Terrence E. Deal and Allen F. Kennedy, whose book, *Corporate Cultures*, had stirred up the organizational behavior community some years before.

Deal and Kennedy had identified myths, rituals, heroes, and celebrations among their corporate culture markers – and those of us who have been in the nonprofit sector a while know just how strong those markers are! Not only do we see them evidenced in management practices, we can also see them in the way we fundraise.

Culture is like the DNA of organizations. The more we know about it, the more we're able to live with its ramifications and predict certain behaviors. And when we attempt to make changes, we certainly have to acknowledge the power of organizational culture.

If Deal and Kennedy took a look at corporate culture as it's reflected in nonprofit fundraising practices, they would certainly identify the following.

If the board hasn't been recruited to raise money, don't expect to change their behavior overnight.

In his autobiography, Lee Iacocca reflected on his experience at Chrysler by saying that to change the culture, you have to change the people. He could have been thinking about the challenge of persuading a board that hasn't been recruited to raise money that they will love fundraising!

To be sure, Iacocca had a distinct advantage: he could fire the vice presidents at Chrysler when he took over, thereby changing the culture. Most of us cannot – and would not want to – "fire" the board.

Even if you now need a board active in fundraising, you still have to respect that this wasn't part of their job description. The first thing to do, obviously, is to change the job description so that "participation in the fund and donor development process" is right up at the top of the list of responsibilities.

The second thing is to be open about that requirement when you recruit new board members.

If adding "participation in the development process" to the list of requirements for board members turns people away – or prompts some to resign – that is one of the first signs of a gradual culture change.

While we lament the loss of board members, often people who resign when the rules change have simply been looking for a reason to leave. As for those who say they don't want to join a board that requires participation in donor and fund development, that's also a dramatic sign you're changing the culture.

It is so much better to be clear at the outset about the culture you're creating, than to have to try to change people's performance once they're on the board. By stating expectations up front, you're no longer perpetuating the old way of thinking. Your culture will begin to change.

Respect the rituals of fundraising, even if you would like to change them as quickly as possible.

In one organization I know, the corporate fundraising volunteer structure was one in which women were team captains and made no calls.

Appalled by the wasted potential of the women who weren't asking for money – many of whom were corporate executives themselves – the new development director sought to reorganize the program. She met with fierce resistance – particularly from some of the women and from the male volunteer head of the program.

It took two years before all teams were integrated with men and women askers. In this situation, the development director modeled the structure she wanted to have in place by setting up a major gifts program in which the chairs, team captains, and askers were men and women who shifted in and out of various roles easily.

Be a careful observer of the way things are celebrated – celebrations are a strong part of the culture.

In one of the many mergers that occurred in medical centers during the past decades, two foundations came together. They couldn't have been more different in nearly every respect of their culture, but it was in the way they celebrated that the contrast was most marked. This applied to both internal (staff) and external (board, donors, community) occasions.

The one, which was larger and more corporate, had done away with many of the little staff parties and celebrations years before, preferring more formal recognition through meetings, flowers, or lunches at local restaurants.

The smaller (but older) foundation had a family culture – potluck lunches, birthday celebrations at the office, and much more "down time" where they boosted each other through informal get-togethers.

It was the same for the recognition and celebration of large gifts and important donors. The one was much more corporate, the other more intimate.

In the end, the more corporate culture predominated and became the culture of the merged foundation.

If your fundraising culture centers on events, it may be difficult to shift people into thinking about how to apply that same effort into developing a program of personal major giving.

In my first development director's job, the organization had nearly one event a month. Although responsibility for the events was shared among the board, specially recruited volunteers, and the auxiliaries, these events were time consuming and, with two or three exceptions, not high revenue producers.

At the same time, the "major gifts" program was a "select mail" effort that asked for gifts of $100 or more.

Over the course of three years, we gradually trimmed and consolidated events, adding a second "blockbuster" that diminished the need for other smaller events, and, through a serendipitous challenge gift, brought the board's understanding of the power of the major ask into sharper focus.

Although the organization still has several events, it has now distinguished itself through both a major capital campaign and an endowment campaign.

Legends play a strong role in the culture of fundraising.

People love to tell the stories of those who, over the history of an organization, have been fearless askers, great event organizers, unexpectedly clever at finding the right way to solicit a resistant donor, or tenacious enough to keep asking even after hearing "no" five or eight times! Referred to as "war stories," people love to tell them and to hear them.

Listen carefully to these stories, because they encapsulate the culture. You'll find flashes of courage, creativity, persistence, and tenacity – and you'll build on the culture if you begin to recognize the new heroes and legends each year. Add them to the list that already exists, and include them in the orientation for new board members.

Many of the legendary askers and organizers are either still involved or still available – strengthen this special part of corporate culture by having them come back and tell their own story.

The way people prepare to ask for a gift -- and the way they ask -- is also indicative of the culture.

Some organizations are very process oriented, requiring training, a team system of soliciting, and perhaps a term of service on the board before an individual becomes a full fledged asker.

In other organizations, no preparation is suggested or encouraged beyond finding out who wants to ask the person, how well they know them, what tools they need, and when they will do it.

Experience tells us that solicitations are more effective when there is *some* preparation. However, trying to force an effective asker into a training session will result in the loss of that asker.

Weigh the need for process carefully when dealing with a culture in which Lone Ranger superstars are used to going out and doing things on their own and with little preparation. If it's working, let them be. Train others who are willing, and gradually the culture will change.

Thanking is a ritual that's part of the culture.

Some organizational cultures are so strong on the thank-you process that they mishandle or over-control it. For example, if the person who *is supposed* to thank certain people is sick or unavailable, some organizations suspend the thank-you process until that individual returns.

Rather than follow this ill-advised approach, it's better to back up the ritual thank-you process with an official one that sends outs the proper receipt or letter from the office.

In working with the culture of thanking in an organization, remember that systems liberate: if you install effective systems that back up the thanking rituals (personal notes, personal phone calls, thankathons, flowers), then you'll still be able to complete the process even if your ritual occasionally breaks down.

In many organizations, the culture of fundraising fails to include the process of donor and fund development.

This may be the most important, and difficult, cultural aspect to alter. In organizations that have focused only on fundraising and not on the larger context of donor and fund development, fundraising is relegated to a few people. Others on the board or committees stand aside and let them do it.

To thrive, the most important cultural shift every organization must make is to create a culture in which development is understood and practiced by everyone – administration, program staff, development staff, board, other volunteers – in all of its intricacies.

There must be a shift from a culture in which fundraising is compartmentalized to a single function – asking for money – to a culture in which development is an inclusive process in which everyone understands that all relationships have potential for enhancing the organization, and everyone plays a role.

To create a culture of philanthropy requires an understanding of philanthropy, development, and fundraising – and the way in which they are interrelated.

Creating a culture of philanthropy isn't easy. It demands new approaches to involving people in development, in marketing the organization internally and externally, and in evaluating and fine-tuning the aspects of both the old and new cultures that are valued.

Creating a culture of philanthropy also requires a respect for the culture that exists, and the aspects of it that need to be retained even as the culture evolves.

Culture and values are tied together, and to address one without embracing the other will lead to friction and resistance.

•••

As Peters and Waterman noted regarding the corporate sector, culture is at once the hardest and softest aspect of an organization. It would seem to be true for the culture of fundraising as well.

Know your organization's culture. Observe it. Listen for it. And listen, especially to the way culture is revealed in such admonitions as: "We tried that once and it didn't work," or "Our donors would *never* respond to *that* kind of an approach."

People who couldn't define their fundraising culture if asked, often reveal it in one simple statement. Respect what you hear and see, and identify those parts that are so attached to the values of your organization that they shouldn't be altered. At the same time, evaluate the way in which the other parts of your culture can and should be modified to accommodate your current vision.

Bob Waterman, in *The Renewal Factor*, talks about how important it is to "surrender the memories" and to take the best and leave the rest. That reflection applies to working with and within the culture of fundraising in your organization.

the mission.

• The website should carry a regularly updated story with pictures of how your organization is making a difference in the lives of the hungry, the homeless, youth leaders or concert goers. And,

• Telephone callers and major gifts solicitors should be equipped with anecdotes that illustrate your work.

You don't have to spend a lot of money to have quality communications.

While those on a tight budget may sigh enviously over the four-color annual report from a local hospital or a major university, there are ways to convey quality and substance without spending thousands of dollars.

In fact, organizations that regularly used to produce glossy color-filled publications are now rethinking that practice in the face of increased criticism from donors who feel this isn't a good use of their money.

There are two basic ways to cut costs and maintain quality. The first is to establish a relationship with a good graphic arts and printing company in your community and ask them to produce your publications as part of their community philanthropy.

This works superbly for the Djerassi Resident Artist Program in Woodside, California. Their annual report is itself a work of art, and is done as a gift. The designer uses the outcome as part of her portfolio, and Djerassi has a magnificent gift for its donors and a tool for outreach and stewardship.

The second way to cut costs and maintain quality is to determine a "look" for all your communications that is classic and not dependent on gloss or color.

One organization did a powerful series of fundraising communications in black and white, with screened photographs of exceptional quality and text that was compelling, succinct, and memorable. Over the years, people came to know and recognize (and respond to) the materials from this organization.

Evaluate the communications you're using, and make changes in the way you communicate that will get people's attention.

If we become too predictable with our mailings, if our website doesn't change for months – or if we fail to package our message in a way that's different enough to capture attention – then we numb all but our most ardent supporters to our message.

Stand back from your communications and ask yourself how you can vary them just enough to maintain consistency while getting the intended market's attention.

Surprise your donors and friends by sending mail other than solicitations. San Francisco Shakespeare Festival sent a thank you Valentine to its donors. Oakland Ballet sent postcards to its donors while on tour. Executive directors often send along an article or white paper they know will be of interest. And a letter from a participant in your programs goes a long way to convince donors of the importance of their gifts.

Know the difference between development and fundraising communications.

Development communications are more like corporate institutional marketing: they convey the case without adding a "sell." They include annual reports, stewardship messages, a program-related video, public relations, and community relations.

Fund raising communications have a "sell" attached: they include remit devices, ways to give through your website, or the telephone solicitor's request.

Development communications are written and designed with the goal of building good will and a relationship; fundraising communications are intended to garner a response. The latter don't necessarily have a long shelf-life in the home or office of the recipient. They're acted on immediately. On the other hand, development communications may be kept, reviewed, and revisited by the recipient.

The goals of these two kinds of communications are related, but different. They will also differ in tone and language. Development communications are written in a more narrative style and will sound and appear more institutional. Fundraising communications will use shorter sentences, more white space, bullet points, bolder images and more active words.

Make time to develop powerful communications.

My secretary used to have a sign on her desk that said, "If it weren't for the last minute, nothing would get done around here." Unfortunately, that often applies to the year-end mailing, the annual report, or the proposal to a new foundation.

Remember that good communications lead to easier fundraising, and regular communications lead to easier renewals and greater reinvestments.

Put sufficient time into the preparation, production, tracking, and evaluation of communications to ensure the best possible results. Use an action plan that spells out the steps in the process and assigns dates and responsibility for completion.

Assemble a group of talented volunteers and have them brainstorm themes and messages. Keep them involved as your "creative committee" and let them use their marketing, writing, or artistic expertise on your behalf.

Few organizations have marketing directors – those that don't can engage volunteers from the community (who are marketing directors elsewhere). While the production of the communications may fall heavily on staff, there are plenty of people in your community who would relish the idea of participating in a creative hour or two every several months.

Set aside professional time, as well, including an occasional day or half day for marketing, planning, evaluation, and idea development. It will be more than worth the time.

Determine your communications goals before you begin developing your communications team or your materials.

Have an idea in mind about how you want to be perceived before you ever work with volunteers or other professionals. While their input is essential and welcomed, if you are the professional it is critical that you know the outcomes you want before you begin.

Perhaps you have done a market survey and know that your visibility is low and the perception of your organization isn't exactly what you'd choose. For example, a community college may be viewed as traditional, essential, and respected – great descriptors all of them. However, officials may want to be known also as innovative, leading edge, exciting, and visionary.

The college, in developing its marketing plan with the help of talented volunteers and professionals, must begin communicating messages that will fulfill their long-term visibility goals.

If you're going to use the Internet for your fundraising communications, be sure you use it in a way that's appropriate for your organization, for the message, and for the potential donor.

There are two approaches to cyber fundraising: solicitations to your known constituency via email (done increasingly among alumni in private secondary and higher education), and dona-

terials. Are the values explicit or implicit? Do people have to work to get beyond the words that describe what you do (" ... provide food for agencies that have feeding programs") to why you do it? ("Hunger hurts. It erodes human dignity, drains human energy, and diminishes human potential.").

Once you have identified the values, the process can begin. Initially, you'll have too many words and ideas, but creative distillation will come later.

Gauge the tolerance of your leadership and the community for a mission statement that overtly conveys values.

If this approach to mission statements represents a sea change for your organization, the benefit of a values statement must be conveyed.

One approach is to explain to your board and volunteers that all voluntary giving (time, money, resources) is based in values; and that in order to become true investors in your work, people must understand what you stand for.

Although corporations may craft short and emotionless mission statements, they convey their values in the way they market products. Automobile ads play to our needs for comfort, power, and distinction. Household product ads imply consequences for not using them. Ice cream ads focus on self-reward as a reason for raiding the freezer at night.

Because fundraising is a marketing process, we have to find ways to roll our values into the principal statement that expresses our mission so it can become a systemic part of the organization's outreach.

Board and staff resistance to this may be keen. At first, you may end up with a mission statement that, rather than used externally to any great extent, is an internal statement of beliefs and a way to focus the organization for decision-making.

Accommodate concerns, and don't force the process. If the context for acknowledgment and discussion of values is encouraged, the mission statement will eventually evolve.

Mission statements are best generated by committee but should be written by one person.

Once the values have been identified, and your staff and board have made some initial attempts at writing a sentence or two, assign the task of expanding (or reducing) the ideas and polishing the phrasing to a good writer who understands your values. This can be a program, administrative, or development staff person, a board member or other volunteer, or a consultant.

The results of "group write" are usually cumbersome and clumsy. In mission statements, economy of language is critical, and each word should have purpose.

Yale University School of Medicine created this short statement for a campaign conducted in the early 1980s when the innovations in biomedical research were just starting: "We are in the midst of one of the most profound intellectual revolutions of all time, the revolution in the biological sciences. Its implications for understanding life processes and for combating disease are boundless. Yale is in the forefront of this revolution."

Although brief, it is rich in values and persuasive in tone.

Once the first draft is ready, test it out on selected internal and external constituencies.

If you send your statement out to everyone, the process will stall. Choose a sampling from board members, major donors, program staff, program and fundraising volunteers, clients, and others currently or formerly close to your organization. You may even have a few versions to try out on them.

Set the criteria for them by explaining the importance of a mission statement that embodies the organization's values. If they were not part of the process that led to the writing of the statement, summarize that process. Provide them with a deadline for giving feedback, and a guideline for responding by phone, fax, mail or email.

You may be delightfully surprised by the ideas that come back through this process. Even one or two can make a big difference. You won't hear back from everyone, but nearly all of those contacted will remember that you asked them. It is a process that promotes ownership of the eventual statement.

Test the statement by checking whether it answers the question, "Why do we exist?"

From the first brainstorming to the final writing, see if the ideas being generated complete the sentence, "We exist because...." For example, "We exist because hunger hurts." "We exist because people need their hands to work, play, love, and talk." "We exist because the biological sciences provide answers to critical life issues."

One community music education organization, searching deeply for its why, answered the challenge this way: "We exist because we cannot imagine a world without music."

If your mission statement is still stuck in "what," you won't be able to finish the sentence, "Why do we exist?"

When the mission statement is tested, be sure it inspires as well as describes.

An occasional outbreak of goosebumps is healthy. It reminds people of the impact of their organization on human needs and potential. The hands statement, quoted earlier, brings goosebumps. Strangely, so does the Yale statement.

A happy outcome of reading such a statement is the sense of "Aha!" The reader feels that she clicks with your values. The basis for a new or enhanced relationship has been discovered.

Remember that mission and vision are not the same, and are often confused.

Mission describes the human or societal need you are meeting. Vision describes what your organization must become to meet the need expressed in your mission.

Jane Stanford, co-founder of Stanford University, wrote the following when the then-regional university was in the depths of financial peril following the death of her husband and the devastating 1906 San Francisco earthquake: "I could see a hundred years ahead, when all the present trials were forgotten ... The children's children's children, coming here from the east, the west, the north and the south."

At the university's Centennial in the early 1990s, her vision of a widely known and mature university was revisited with a sense of pride and fulfillment.

Not everyone is comfortable with values statements, so keep a "what" statement in reserve.

Just as those close to your organization may resist the values thrust of this type of mission statement, so, too, may some of your funders or other external constituents.

Keep a "what" statement handy. In fact, most mission statements written in the way described here are short paragraphs followed by longer statements that describe what the organization does. A funder may only wish to read the more traditional descriptive information.

Use it or lose it. And revisit it annually.

Adapt it, play with it, draw from it, be creative with it. Rearrange the words for various purposes: brochures, tag lines on stationery, donor thank you receipts, remit envelopes, signage in your administrative offices or where you see your clients. Test drive it annually, and if it still works leave it alone. If it doesn't, fix it by reviewing this process.

Writing it is not enough — you have to live the values, too.

A statement behind a receptionist's desk is nice, but living the mission is better. Express your organization's values in what you do, how you do it, the decisions you make, and the way you treat people internally and in the community. Keep the mission fresh inside the organization.

This will help prevent "mission drift," a problem that occurs when the board becomes more consumed with the institution's internal needs than with the external need that is being addressed.

•••

Creating or revising your mission statement is one excellent exercise for rekindling values and getting board members inspired.

A mission statement that tells "why" invites those who share your values to become more involved. It signals your community that you understand your true mission. It inspires your board and helps prevent "mission drift." It provides the values base for tough decision-making, and it is the source of other expressions of your mission that you'll develop for ongoing fundraising and community outreach.

The time and patience required for the process are well worth it.

6

UNDERSTANDING THE MOTIVATIONS OF MAJOR DONORS

Motivated major donors. We want them. We need them. We strive to keep them. And yet, we find ourselves too often frustrated because we don't have them, still need them, or, worse, we've lost them.

Much has been written about major donor motivation. Sweeping generalizations profile the most likely major donors and so we find, in our communities, that we're all turning to the same people because they fit the profile.

Lists for feasibility studies for capital campaigns contain the same names, year after year. In the back of performing arts programs, in annual reports and newsletters from social service organizations, and in the publications of independent schools and colleges, we see the same names. Over-solicited, these "most likely to be major donors" members of our communities become increasingly resistant as donor fatigue sets in.

So, what's the answer? If the profile of the major-rated "Everydonor" is so proven, yet so exhausted, where do we turn to find the new major donor -- one who will be so sparked by the mission and impact of our organization that she will make (and renew) a significant investment?

And, as important, how do we create the conditions in which even experienced donors will be more motivated and excited about the opportunities we offer them to invest through us in our communities?

Two obviously emerging major donor groups are women, and the thirty- and forty-something men and women who have done well in technology or related industries. But, the purpose of this chapter isn't to identify likely groups, it is to pinpoint the motivations of major donors that cross group lines. Our purpose here is to provide some new ideas to help all organizations venture off the well-worn paths and find new doors to open.

Here, then, are the most important things to know about the motivations of major donors.

The old generalizations about motivation need to be rethought.

While recognition, peer pressure, guilt, the quest for immortality, and other traditional motivations may still be present, it's important to realize that a younger generation of donors and the rising role of women in philanthropy have added some new motivations that can prove beneficial to organizations who understand them.

Thirty-somethings and forty-somethings who are very successful have been, for the most part, significant creators of the ideas, products, and services that have made them wealthy. They're used to being involved in the creation, implementation, and evaluation of projects: they respond to outcomes. They want to be involved.

In some communities, the scions of the wealthy families have departed from their philanthropic traditions and are directing their money towards programs with high social impact rather than those with high social recognition.

It is the same with many emerging women philanthropists. All the recent studies about women's philanthropy distinguish it from men's philanthropy with one common conclusion: women get involved first, and then give. They are less apt to respond to peer pressure; more apt to follow their own hearts.

The younger generation of donors shares some of that same profile, and are also less apt to give for recognition only. In fact, some shy away from recognition entirely.

Understanding these needs in donors may also be another way to energize tired donors.

Three basic motivations are connection, concern, capacity.

We focus on capacity, when we should concentrate on connection and concern about (or interest in) the mission the organization serves.

Too often, organizations think they can identify their future major donors by combing Forbes (for the 400), Fortune (for the 500), or their own local organizations for their lists of high-end donors.

Those lists are an aid only if they bear names of people who have a connection with your organization or who are known to be concerned about your mission.

Spend your time looking first for the connection or the concern. If someone is concerned (preferably passionate) about the need you're meeting in the community, then you can bring her closer by building the relationship and creating the connection.

If the relationship already exists between the prospective donor and your organization or someone involved with your organization, but the concern or interest is unknown or weak, you can inform and involve him around the mission.

If the capacity to give is large, and the connection and concern are solid, it is a winning combination. Without the connection and the concern, capacity alone will not a major donor make!

And, make sure you haven't relegated your existing major donors into "giving categories" instead of into categories that identify what they think about and what they care about.

Motivation is an *internal* issue — what organizations provide is the right *external* environment for that motivation to flourish.

One spin on motivation theory is that you cannot motivate people: they are already motivated, and your job is to find out what motivates them and construct the right environment in which their motivation will flourish. With newer philanthropists, this is especially true.

The motivation comes from within. Something happens when you see a donor connect with the values, mission, and vision of your organization. Sometimes it's as though there's an audible "click." Suddenly, the desires of the organization and the desires of the prospective donor are wedded.

Getting the donor to that point requires patience and a great deal of listening. Hear what the prospect is asking and saying. Watch what peaks her interest, and when her interest flags. Observe to whom she gravitates at social and educational gatherings. Reflect on the questions she asks.

All of these factors construct the picture of the person's motivation, and help the organization respond with integrity and good intent to help the current or new donor achieve fulfillment and the organization to realize its goals.

Motivation grows out of values.

This is indisputable. Part of the "click" mentioned above is the sound of values matching. The prospect realizes that, for example, this is the educational philosophy that will produce future citizens of which the community will be proud, or this is the approach to programs for developmentally disabled adults that insures the most dignity, or this is the dance company that most closely reflects the diversity the donor seeks in the arts and in the community.

Values are best conveyed in programs and actions. Words alone aren't persuasive. A major donor will be motivated when she sees her values manifested.

Keeping existing major donors connected with the values also maintains motivation.

And, involving current major donors with the cultivation of prospective major donors gives them opportunities to examine and convey shared values.

Motivation is ignited by the passion that comes from involvement and belief in the mission.

The age of the passive philanthropist is ending. As the face of philanthropy changes, so does its quest. An interest in outcomes is replacing a need for rewards. While recognition is still important, the way in which it is provided is changing. It is more mission-connected.

Those who benefit, those who are served, those who are grateful for the programs and services: these are the individuals with whom thoughtful major philanthropists want to be connected. It is they who provide the passion that motivates continued giving. Passion is essential, and passion is fueled by involvement. It begins with the board, many of whom may be major donors.

Each board meeting needs a "mission moment" in which a client, patron, or person connected with or served by the organization shares his observations and appreciation.

Research may give clues about motivation, but the only truly reliable resource is the donor.

Get to know your major prospects and donors. More importantly, get to know as many of your donors — major or not — as you can. See them all as having potential to give a large gift at some time or to connect you with those who can. If you're fortunate enough to have research capability at your organization, use it as a baseline.

Validate it through conversation and involvement. Throw out the old paradigms and be open to those on whom no research exists. Inexperienced donors need to feel supported by an organization that understands their need for information, involvement and, in many cases, time.

The goal of good stewardship is to keep the donor motivated.

Stewardship, which is the ongoing relationship with a donor based on mutual respect for both the source and impact of the gift, is perhaps the most important function in the development process. It is critical to maintaining major donor motivation.

So many institutions have lost major donors through their failure to maintain a values and mission-based relationship with their donors. They wine, dine and solicit prospects and then, once the gift is secured, place the new donor into the donor file and close it up.

For them, the transaction is over. But, for the donor, the relationship is just beginning. Honoring the donor, and his motivation, is the key to effective stewardship. Motivation is stimulated by knowing that the shared values of the donor and the institution are being advanced. Stewardship is the vehicle for conveying that information.

Corporate and foundation motivation is different from individual motivation, but remember that corporations and foundations are run by individuals.

Although corporations and foundations may be motivated by more complex factors in their giving (perception as corporate citizens, investing in a local or national agenda), remember they are run by individuals.

When a corporation or foundation becomes a major donor, chances are it's because your organization matches the guidelines or fulfills their community commitment to a particular population, service, need, or ideal.

Most often, the process for obtaining a gift is relatively impersonal, requiring a certain level of objective application within funding guidelines. However, during the gift-seeking process and afterwards, as stewardship is implemented, the motivations of decision-making individuals should be watched and responded to. Chances are, you'll end up with a continuing and deeper relationship.

Motivated donors must be linked with motivated volunteers.

The increasing trend in universities, hospitals, and other larger organizations to use staff-soliciting only is unfortunate. The presence of a volunteer, motivated by the values and mission of the organization and giving of his time to meet with a potential donor, cannot be over-valued. The peer ask continues to be the most effective, and the most motivating, in major gifts programs.

This doesn't in any way undermine the training, effectiveness, or knowledge of development staff: It's merely a plea for the continued involvement of motivated volunteers - often with staff - in the cultivation and solicitation of major gifts.

Ultimately, the most motivated major donors will self-solicit.

This concept, first introduced to me many years ago by a motivated and effective volunteer at Stanford University, Bill

Kimball, has repeatedly proven true.

When the environment is established in which a prospective donor's motivations can flourish, and when the prospect is connected with volunteers who themselves are motivated and share the prospect's values, the prospect begins to self-solicit.

Presented with an array of opportunities to act on his values, the prospect begins an internal dialogue in which the gift is considered and "solicited."

While few donors will actually step forward without being asked, the self-solicit ensures that — when the prospect is asked — the ensuing transaction will be characterized by excitement, energy, and commitment.

It is the same with those who are already committed as major donors. They will renew and increase their gifts if a motivating environment surrounds them. The challenge to those who ask is to stay so connected to the prospect or donor that the right time to ask becomes obvious.

The motivation accelerates, the involvement increases, and the desire to invest becomes clear. Seize the moment: it will reap rewards for the donor, and for the organization.

•••

Ultimately, major donor motivation is as varied as the donors themselves. Learn to look for the unique aspects of each current and potential donor: his values, interests, connections, and what he cares about. While some aspects of the traditional profiles still hold true, there's so much more to consider.

A broader view of motivation will bring a broader base of major donors, and among them will be the "new philanthropists:" those who are mercifully free of donor fatigue.

And, you just might find a cure for donor fatigue among the major donors that everyone seeks. They're all looking increasingly for continued involvement, values-based feedback, and opportunities to make a difference.

7

KEEPING YOUR PROSPECT PIPELINE FULL

All organizations know the importance of keeping the pipeline filled with potential donors. What they often don't know is where to find the names to put into the pipeline.

We've all been to meetings where the development committee or board members are pressed into coming up with the names of friends, neighbors, and others, and there's probably not a person reading these words who hasn't been required to review lists of donors from other organizations. This is particularly true during capital campaigns or just before an annual drive. People hit the panic button: where can we find more prospects?

Effective fundraising management includes keeping the pipeline full at all times, not just before or during capital or annual campaigns. Potential donors, or prospects, should be continually identified, qualified, strategically managed, cultivated, and eventually solicited. But, like so many aspects of our complex profession, this is easier in the saying than in the doing.

Prospect identification is a key part of the three-prong responsibility of development officers and volunteers:

1) Soliciting and stewarding current donors,
2) Identifying and cultivating prospects, and
3) Maintaining the infrastructure to support our efforts.

Somehow, wedged between what many call "front line fundraising" and the maintenance of staffing and systems to support the development program, the middle prong — identifying and cultivating prospects — often gets left behind until the shortage is felt. It's like running out of gas: if you wait until the warning light appears, and you have no source of fuel in sight, it's going to be a tough journey.

Here's what you should know about identifying prospective donors or spotting current donors who can be upgraded.

Analyze your own database before reviewing the lists of other organizations.

One performing arts organization, in its 10th successful season (but just beginning a formal individual giving program after years of solid foundation and some corporate funding) was frustrated in its search for potential donors.

The organization gathered lists from similar arts organizations and board members carefully perused the names to see if anyone was familiar with the people or could make a secondary connection through a mutual friend. Additionally, they reviewed business journals, newspapers, and other sources for potential names of people with wealth they could begin cultivating.

A consultant, called in to assist with the formation of their development program, asked how many people from their own subscriber and single-ticket buyer list were already donors and how many they had identified as good prospects. The response: it hadn't occurred to the organization to review its own subscriber and ticket buyer list as a source of prospects.

When the board and staff finally did, their review yielded great results. Not only did the organization tap into an already-connected, ready-made prospect list, it realized it had a large potential in the number of subscribers who were already giving but had never been formally solicited or properly acknowledged.

The result: the organization found itself with a long list of subscriber-prospects; it began serious stewardship of these people; and it launched a successful subscriber-giving program that continues to this day.

Computerized databases, essential tools today for nonprofit management, have their downside: we tend to "put people into the database" and leave them there. In the time of 3 x 5 cards for donors and prospects, there was a certain tactile interaction with those names. Cards were shuffled, touched and sorted — each representing an individual. Now, with our printouts and reports, we've become numbed to the reality of what each name represents: someone who is or could be connected, involved, and grown as a donor and advocate. Prospectors, mine your own lists first!

Not all prospects are prospects for first-time gifts: think, as well, of prospects for upgraded gifts who are lying untended in your database.

Hank Rosso, founder of The Fund Raising School, used to teach his students that there are four types of donors: impulsive, habitual, thoughtful, and careful.

Impulsive donors are usually first-time donors — they like your letter, your event, the article about you in the paper, or the person who calls and asks them. They haven't yet thought deeply about the values involved or how they would fit in.

If these donors renew, the danger is they'll become *habitual* donors, giving year after year at the same level and telling their friends, "Yes, I always give $100 at Christmas to the Lung Association."

This can go on for years, unless effort is put into converting them into *thoughtful* donors: those who give a great deal of thought to their gift, matching it to the values the organization advances, the needs it is addressing, and their own satisfaction as donors with the results they perceive.

Finally, they may make a *careful* gift — literally, a gift full of care. It can be a special, major, or planned gift, but it is often transformational in its impact on the donor and the organization.

Organizations that have a large number of habitual donors should consider creating a "transition team" among their board or development committee members to give them an assignment that is both strategic and tactical.

The transition team analyzes the database and identifies those donors who are stuck at a certain level. These names are reviewed, considered as a separate prospect list, and given special attention, information, stewardship, and outreach.

If done well, these donors come to understand that their involvement can make an even greater impact if they increase their gift. Most habitual givers haven't been truly connected to the mission. The job of the transition team is to make that connection.

Remember that systems liberate: have a good one in place for prospect identification, qualification, and development of a strategy for getting the first gift or upgrading a habitual donor.

There's nothing random about developing a solid prospect base. There may be windfalls — someone brings in an "A" list that you know will be a rich resource for you — but most of the fully functioning pipelines work because of the systematic approach taken by those managing them.

Prospect identification sessions — looking at your own lists or those of other organizations — should take place bi-monthly or quarterly. Those involved should include board members, former board members, other volunteers, and staff.

In addition to review sessions, which should be done only after lists have been put into a clean, legible, and consistent form, establish a regular process for gathering new names. At all board, committee, and staff meetings, provide a sheet of paper on top of the meeting packet that simply says, "Since our last meeting, I've met or thought of the following people who would be interested in our organization."

If each person provides two or three names each session, imagine how your list would grow. Using this approach (rather than, "Since our last meeting, I've met or thought of the following people who have lots of money") board members begin thinking of people with an interest or concern about the issues and values of the organization, and they can begin envisioning how they might connect them to the organization.

When a critical mass (100 to 200) has been gathered, these names should be reviewed at a formal session.

If your organization has an active development committee, consider creating a subcommittee for prospect development.

In addition to systems and strategies, it's good to have one group in charge of prospect development. They gather the names that come in. They work with staff to "merge/purge" the new names against existing lists. They create the lists that board, other volunteers, and staff will review, and they process and collate the results of that review.

After an event, they review attendees against the list of prospects and donors and make sure all are included. They guard against the empty pipeline. They then give their information to the larger development committee, charged with implementing a cultivation and fundraising strategy.

Keep all prospect review sessions confidential.

There's nothing worse than having a prospect identification or review session turn into a gossip session. This aspect of "prospecting" is one reason people don't like to participate.

Set up your sessions so that lists are reviewed silently, and names are presented on forms that are easy to use. Some of the information you want on these prospects can be provided by yes/no boxes, and by providing coded giving levels (A, B, C, D).

While the narrative comments are always the most interesting, make it easy for the evaluators. Chances are, they'll be more apt to write comments if you have given them some boxes to check or multiple choices to circle.

When reviewers have finished, they can turn in their lists in an envelope with their name on the outside, and leave the session. It's then up to the prospect development committee to review, and discuss confidentially, the completed lists.

From this information, strategies for approaching prospects or upgrading donors are developed.

Keep the pipeline full of likely prospects -- prune the deadwood regularly.

Lists are not sacred. They should be culled, reviewed, cut, cleaned up and names deleted on a regular basis. While there may be safety in numbers in some situations, the prospect pipeline is not necessarily one of them unless all the "numbers" are likely prospects.

Some organizations seem to hang on to lists forever. They don't let go of dead people, duplicate names, or changed names. It is as if they do not read their own lists.

Just like a New Year's Resolution, pick a day every year when you print out the whole list, look at the activity reports, check against the returned mail reports (that pile in the back of the work room that no one has time for), and look at the lapsed donors.

If you hate to lose anyone, then send out a special mailing -- asking people if they want to stay on your mailing list. Don't be afraid of the answer -- knowing that someone wants off your list is better prospect relations than keeping her on the list if your mail is irritating her. Make room for a fresh batch of names.

If you have a newsletter, use it as a way of finding new prospects.

Run a box in every newsletter asking your readers to suggest names of people who might like to know more about the organization and receive your newsletter. You might be pleasantly surprised.

Include a box readers can check regarding whether or not their name can be used when contacting the person or sending the newsletter. If it's all right to use their name, send the first copy of the newsletter in an envelope and include a note that says, "At the suggestion of Gracie Martin, we are sending you this issue of our newsletter. She felt you'd be interested in our organization and the needs it is meeting in our community."

If Gracie does not want her name used, send the newsletter in an envelope with a note from the executive director or board chair. The note can say "It has come to our attention that you're interested in programs that address community needs similar to those we're involved with, and we're taking this opportunity to let you know more about our organization."

If you aren't sure whether you have enough prospects to reach your annual or capital goal, do a gift range chart early in the planning phase.

The gift range chart is one of the handiest tools in fundraising. By establishing the range of gifts needed to reach an annual or capital goal, the number of gifts at each step of the range, and the prospect-to-donor ratio at each level, you can get a pretty quick picture of whether you have enough prospects to reach your intended goal.

One organization, considering a capital campaign of $1.5 million was happily (and successfully) able to up its goal to $2.7 million when it did a detailed donor and prospect analysis.

The organization first did a gift range chart for a $1.5 million campaign, but found that their own prospect and donor base, when formulated in the prospect-to-gift ratio, had much greater potential.

The converse can also be true. Many organizations have had to lower the goals of their annual campaigns when they began putting actual numbers of prospects against the needed gifts on a gift range chart. This tool should be used in all fundraising planning.

Involve existing donors in prospect review and development.

Those who are already enthusiastic donors can be great sources of names of other potential donors. While we do this routinely with board members, remember to do it with your other key donors as well. It extends their sense of involvement, and they often are willing to help cultivate and solicit the individuals they recommend.

Be sure the process of prospect identification, review, strategy development, and cultivation is characterized by confidentiality, sensitivity, and a values-inspired approach.

We're not looking for "pigeons" whose arms we're either going to hit or twist — this vocabulary is inappropriate even in the most confidential circles of your organization. Voluntary giving is a form of service to the community — it is the way people invest in and strengthen institutions that create excellent communities.

At every step of the way, development professionals and leadership volunteers need to convey the dignity of the process. From the way in which names are gathered, handled, respected, and reviewed, through the cultivation and solicitation itself, you will find many more people willing to help you find prospects and upgrade donors if the process has integrity.

Assure people that their name won't be used without their permission, that all names submitted go through a review process -- one in which they can be involved. Let them know you respect them, the people they suggest, and their relationship with each other.

One organization was unable to convince any board member to provide names because the process used previously wasn't discreet, systematic, or well-explained. It took years to build their confidence that they would not be compromised again.

•••

The search for prospects needn't be a daunting activity if you create and implement systems and structure to keep the process continually rolling — and if you remember that our sector provides untold benefits to its communities and its citizens. When you develop new names for potential involvement, you are laying the foundation for increased community impact and personal fulfillment for donors.

8

CULTIVATING YOUR DONORS

It's no secret that a principal factor in the successful solicitation of major donors is appropriate cultivation.

Cultivation, as you know, usually involves lunches, dinners, events, materials, tours, and other timely and purposeful interactions between prospects and staff and volunteers.

But effective cultivation isn't a random series of unconnected activities: it is strategic, systematic, coordinated, and part of the overall solicitation plan for an initial or renewed gift.

The quality of your cultivation and follow-through has a major effect on the ease and success of the eventual solicitation. Here are the most important things to know about the process of donor cultivation.

Cultivation is a partnership involving board members, volunteers, donors, and staff.

Staff choreographs and participates in opportunities for board members and other volunteers to meet and talk with prospective donors.

But volunteers must make themselves available for regularly planned events (concerts, receptions, auctions, lectures, tours) to which prospective donors will be invited. They also need to be willing to initiate or participate in special cultivation activities planned with specially selected prospects.

Current donor-investors also play a role in cultivation. Their participation in particular events provides opportunities for donors to become advocates with prospects about the importance they attach to their investment in your organization.

Cultivation is strategic.

While we tend to think of cultivation as parties and events during which we introduce potential donors to the people and mission of our organization, we must also think of it strategically. Parties and events, without follow-up based on a cogent cultivation plan, are ineffective.

Cultivation planning takes two forms: general and specific. Have a strategic plan for each.

General cultivation is comprised of scheduled events to which board and staff members bring people with interest in and potential for giving. Specific cultivation activities are those geared for special prospects, those who may or may not also attend regularly scheduled activities or events.

Both types of cultivation are geared to the interests of the prospective donor. Both require follow-through.

Cultivation is systematic.

After any kind of event or activity, a follow-through plan ensures a stronger connection with those who attended. Good follow-through techniques include immediate addition of names to your mailing list and thank-you letters that convey the success of the event or program to those who attended. Personal phone calls from board members or event committee members to patrons of the event also have a considerable impact.

At cultivation or recognition events, assign a board member to each table (unless of course the table has been bought by someone for a group and is completely filled). Provide board members and other key volunteers with confidential lists and short biographies of those at their table.

Also, if some of those attending an event are part of your top prospect pool (or are already large donors), be sure a board member is assigned to look after those individuals at the event.

Where tables are hosted, a member of the board or dinner committee can circulate graciously at an appropriate interval among the seated guests with a warm welcome on behalf of your organization.

Cultivation should be coordinated.

All staff and volunteer interaction with prospective or current donors needs to be reported to the central coordinating officer of your organization — either the development director or, if there's no development department, the executive director or board chair.

There are several reasons for this.

First, staff may have information that's critical to any conversation with the prospect (for example, previous gifts, previous outreach).

Second, the prospect may be "on hold" for another opportunity or reason not known to the volunteers, and pursuit of a gift at this time would be inappropriate.

Third, the prospect may already have been assigned to another volunteer and the duplicate effort would send a confusing signal to the prospect.

Finally, the volunteer (or staff person) may benefit from special information about the organization, for example, information about one of the organization's special projects that may relate to a prospect's particular concern.

An Action Update Form or other easily filled out, faxable form (or e-mail connection) will make such coordination painless.

Cultivation shouldn't be limited to large gift prospects only.

During the year, include a cultivation component in the program for every activity to which the community is invited. While this may seem obvious, countless organizations miss opportunities to showcase their impact to an unfamiliar audience.

Be sure that everyone who attends a gala event leaves the event with increased knowledge about the sponsoring organization. Too often, people will comment about a great event but, when pressed for the sponsoring organization, won't remember.

A brief presentation, materials at the table, a packet given to attendees as they exit the event: these will serve as tools for beginning to build a relationship with those not yet aware of or connected to your organization.

Not all cultivation involves personal interaction.

Simply providing information is another way to cultivate prospects. Your newsletter, for instance, is a form of cultivation, and can be used very effectively for this purpose. Evaluate it and be sure it is conveying the message you most want your readers to receive.

- Does it convey the impact and results of your programs, or does it focus on your needs?
- Does it portray — in words and photographs — the kinds of people you're serving in your programs?
- Does it balance volunteer information, donor recognition, and program impact? Or does it overemphasize the social aspect

of your organization and show, instead, too many photographs of your parties?

Newsletters are one form of non-personal cultivation, but there are others. If you have a special program which is of known interest to the prospect, have the program staff person prepare a "white paper" relating your local program to an article in a magazine or newspaper that focuses on a local, national or international need that your organization is addressing.

A family service organization focused on its child abuse prevention program with a group of donors. An excellent article on the importance of child abuse prevention education was pulled from a major national newspaper. The position paper prepared by the staff person focused on what the local family service agency was doing to address this issue of national concern.

The newspaper article and the white paper were sent to prospects with a note emphasizing the importance of the local action in this area of broad concern. It was an excellent cultivation tool.

Cultivation, with or without systematic planning, can also occur unexpectedly.

Favorable press coverage of an event or a program will heighten awareness among potential donors of your organization and its mission. Enthused board members and other volunteers are often informal advocates, unwittingly arousing great interest among those with whom they interact socially and professionally.

The largest gift from an individual (nearly a half million dollars) to a campaign for a social service agency was made anonymously by an individual who became interested in the organization because of the enthusiasm and advocacy of one of its staff members.

The donor had no prior connection to the organization but, over time, respected the commitment of the staff member and shared the basic values and mission of the agency.

In another case, a bequest in excess of $1 million was received by a children's services agency from a woman whose only experience with the organization was through a neighbor who was a dedicated volunteer and would share stories of her experiences with her friend.

Both of these gifts were the result of a relationship with an individual who was committed to an organization, but were not part of a deliberate cultivation plan.

While it's important to cultivate, know when to ask.

The quality of your cultivation and follow-through has a major effect on the ease and success of the eventual solicitation. Those responsible for monitoring the cultivation of key prospects must recognize signs that a prospect is getting close to the point where she can be asked for a gift.

Cultivation, because it is pleasant and painless, can easily become a consuming activity. But continuing cultivation staves off the inevitable: asking for a gift. You must watch the prospect for signs of growing interest and willingness to be involved. If she's asking, "How can I help?" or "What can I do for this project?" or "Is it possible to get more involved?", then you have done a great job.

Most signals aren't so obvious. Meaningful conversations to assess the degree of interest should be part of every cultivation activity. As the relationship progresses, keep the evaluation constant. When you feel the time is right with an individual, ask.

Cultivation of corporations and foundations is different from cultivation of individuals in one major respect.

sonally during the year.

Objections to this process are often strong: board and staff leaders cite lack of time, lack of necessity, and the idea that board members don't need to be solicited personally since they're "part of the family." But that is precisely why they need to be asked personally for their gift.

The time spent in that one hour (or less), listening to their concerns and enthusiasm, is critical to deepening the board member's involvement. It is a renewal point as their motivations and needs are reviewed, and it's a modeling exercise for them in how to ask for a gift face-to-face.

Even though not all board members will make a "major" gift (at whatever level you've set as major), all board members are "major donors" and should be offered the time and respect other major donors receive.

Be sure all board members have been asked to give before they're asked to solicit others.

This principle is so proven it doesn't require much discussion. Believe it. Because inclusive language (for example, "join with us," "be part of this vital program") is such a critical part of a successful solicitation, it's very important that all board members who ask for gifts can, with authenticity, say "join me." It's also very important that board members are able to say with comfort, "Our entire board is supporting the organization and its work."

Involve them in the development process before requiring them to fundraise.

Too many personal solicitation programs neglect the importance of the development process. Succumbing to the widely-held notion that "development" is just a nice word for "fundraising," they overlook the importance of the steps that precede asking.

The planning and organization of a major gifts program should involve six steps before solicitation: identify/qualify, develop initial strategy, cultivate, involve, evaluate, assign. Then the prospect should be personally solicited.

Afterwards, there are three more steps in which board members can become involved: follow-through and acknowledgment, stewardship of the gift and the giver, and renewal.

When board members get involved in the first six steps, they're much more apt to want to be involved in the seventh. And, when they're also involved in the last three steps, they begin to see the cycle and flow of development, not just the one-shot act of fundraising. Their comfort level rises.

Emphasize the importance of developing donor relationships.

When organizations engage boards not just in "fund development" but in "donor development," the focus shifts appropriately from the organization to the donor. The entire language of development and fundraising becomes donor-centered, and the needs and interests of prospective or renewing donors become the framework of the solicitation.

Fear and cynicism decline, and phrases like "arm-twisting," "hitting someone up" (or other regrettable references to inviting investment in an organization that's solving problems or enhancing the quality of life) disappear. And, with their disappearance, much of the apprehension about fundraising (including fear of rejection and perception as a beggar) wanes.

In solicitations, board members hear the donor's needs and

concerns, rather than focusing on their own worries. They share their enthusiasm about the organization's impact and results, rather than laboring over the organization's financial needs. The act of asking becomes not one of pressure, but of release, as the donor and the asker forge an investment strategy to accomplish mutual goals in the community through the efforts of an established or proposed organization.

Train and coach.

Offer formal training — attended by all board members whether they'll be askers or not — as part of the preparation for the major gifts personal solicitation program. A balanced training session will include elements that inspire, motivate, and inform.

Case histories or personal testimonials from those who have participated in or benefited from the program inspire volunteer solicitors and give heart to the appeal.

Motivation to ask is increased by presenting current and compelling documentation regarding the need the organization is meeting in the community, observable impact of the programs, and the importance of increasing its outreach and service.

Adding a model solicitation demonstration to the training session also helps; so does role-play. After the formal training, most volunteers will also benefit from coaching in specific techniques just prior to their calls.

As part of their training, give them tools. Written materials, videos, audio tapes, photographs, explanations of programs, answers to the most likely objections they will hear: all of these form the "tool box" that helps board members build their confidence to interact with a potential donor.

Find out what they want. Ask them what information they

need to feel confident about answering questions and objections. Have them meet with program staff to review program materials: they'll learn for themselves, and be able to share that information with others.

Also, equip board member solicitors with the information about the prospect they'll need to make a well-placed ask. They should know the person's giving history, their interests and involvement, and what other organizations they are involved with. Remember to convey only information that is public knowledge: knowing too much about someone can make that person feel awkward and resistant.

Emphasize the importance of being themselves and natural in a solicitation.

While masterful solicitors have some traits in common, most of which can be acquired through the steps stated above, a major value in having board involvement in the asking process is the delight of seeing so many different and natural styles.

Donors dislike "slick" askers. The whole rationale for a peer solicitation is that the person being asked feels comfortable with the person asking. Encourage board members to be themselves, while striving to demonstrate the qualities of effective askers: well-prepared, while not appearing rehearsed; excellent listener; able to handle objections because they are well-prepared; willing to admit they don't have an answer; committed; enthusiastic; focused on the purpose of the meeting, and comfortable with the process of asking.

Team every board member with another board member or staff person for the call.

Pair an experienced board member or knowledgeable staff

member (program, administrative, or development) with a board member who's just getting comfortable with the process (or with the organization).

Team solicitations are more effective than one-on-one asks, and they also raise the comfort level of the less experienced asker. The donor doesn't feel "double teamed" — in fact, many report that a team of two individuals with whom they can converse and interact is more comfortable than a one-on-one meeting which may become awkward if conversation lags.

Team solicitations should be well-planned before the visit to avoid confusion over which person carries which portion of the solicitation. Also, it's a good idea to let the prospect know that two people will be coming, and to explain who each person is.

As a staff person, be willing to play a key role in setting up the appointment and preparing the board members for success.

This is a team effort, and sometimes the only role of the staff person is before or after the ask.

The development officer needn't accompany the board member in order to feel involvement and responsibility for the success of the call. The development officer will be involved in: setting up the appointment ("I'm calling at the request of ... to ask when it would be convenient for ... to meet with ... to discuss ..."), preparing prospect profiles, sending out a "pre-solicitation" letter or packet, providing follow up information and acknowledgement.

The partnership between board and staff -- and the feeling of mutual trust and respect -- is vital to raising board member comfort with the fundraising process.

Shed old attitudes about fundraising throughout the organi-

**zation and bring board members closer to the program and
its results.**

All fundraising requires a deliberate retirement of the "tin cup"
attitude that guided far too many nonprofits for decades. It was
based on the idea that nonprofits were "needy" organizations.

The new principle which should guide nonprofit asking —
and help relieve some of the objections and anxiety of board members and other volunteers — is this: nonprofits require community support because they meet needs, not because they have
needs.

This innovation in attitude removes one of the biggest ob-
stacles to asking, the fear of being perceived as a beggar. When
this attitude can be conveyed, askers find themselves focusing
on results, not needs. They can speak comfortably and enthusi-
astically about the impact the organization is having in the community.

This requires much more interaction between the board and
program staff. Some of the administrative filters may have to be
removed so that program staff can communicate directly with
board members about their program results and funding opportunities.

**Make sure each board meeting reinforces program results,
the value of board member involvement in development and
fundraising, and has time set aside for appreciation of
efforts.**

Getting board members involved in the personal solicitation
of major gifts requires a cultural change in some organizations,
including the identification of the link between successful asks
and program strength, and the recognition of efforts made by
board members to get out in the community and advocate for

the organization.

Keep board members close to the "product" by including a program presentation (not a report) at all board meetings. Not all board members may become successful askers, but all board members can participate in a successful development process.

And, be sure to celebrate even small wins. In one national campaign, volunteers were reluctant to get started with their calls. But when the organization began sending out certificates to those who made their first personal face-to-face calls, motivation and results increased dramatically.

Whimsical, informal, and highly prized, these certificates identified the recipient as someone who had "earned his spurs" by making his first call. As a motivation tool, it worked.

•••

The only failure in fundraising is not asking. The personal meeting opens the prospect's mind and heart to your organization and, even if a gift isn't given at that time, the process opens the door to establish and maintain communication. At some later time, a gift may be forthcoming.

Always thank board members for making the effort, and encourage them to maintain the relationship even when no gift is realized from the effort.

Ultimately, if the board member cannot overcome his reluctance, don't force the issue. There are plenty of important steps in donor development on which the individual can focus: you may end up creating a smaller board team that makes the ask.

Concentrate on getting your board involved in donor development. Chances are, if they get really involved, they will forget their fear of fundraising.

10

THE DYNAMICS OF A SOLICITATION CALL

The time has come. You know it's right. All signs point to it. Your prospect is ready to be asked.

Getting to this point has taken time, cultivation, the discovery of mutual values and interests, probably a few "test conversations" about becoming a donor in your organization, and a great deal of listening and waiting for the right opportunity. So far, so good. Now, you want to make sure the solicitation call goes well.

The right dynamics will ensure that the prospect's experience is positive, and that the desired transformation - from interested prospect to committed donor - takes place.

The key thing to remember about the solicitation call is its paradoxical nature: for the organization seeking the investment, it's the culmination of the process; but for the prospective donor, it's the commencement of a long-term relationship. At least it should be.

If it is viewed by the organization as the long-anticipated end point ("We got the gift at last!"), rather than the beginning of a deeper and more valued relationship ("We see so many ways we can involve the person further."), then chances are that's what it will be. And, if the organization returns to that same individual a year or more later, hoping for a similar investment, it may be disappointed.

Remember that giving is transformational, not just transactional. I'll focus here on the more transactional side of the process, but its undergirding is deeply attached to the transformational nature of giving. Giving transforms prospects into donors and then, depending on the impact of the gift, transforms programs, institutions, individuals, and entire communities.

To lose sight of the transformational nature of giving is to let go of the values basis of all philanthropy, development, and fundraising.

Here's what you need to do to ensure that the solicitation call is donor-focused, values-based, and well executed.

Be certain the timing is right.

Watch for signals from the prospect: deepening interest, probing questions, greater involvement, and the willingness to comment and counsel on your programs and projects.

Hear your prospects when they speak of their own personal circumstances (recently-sold business or home, an inheritance they want to do something with, appreciated property, tax issues, the last child graduating from college). They may be offering clues that the time is right to make a major current or planned investment in your organization.

Life, as has been said, is all a matter of timing. It is true for solicitations as well.

Be prepared.

The Boy Scouts' motto is a good one for nonprofit volunteers and managers - particularly when it comes to the dynamics of the solicitation call. There's no substitute for good preparation.

The introduction of "moves management" strategies by David Dunlop of Cornell University a decade or more ago has made good managers and their volunteers more conscious of the natural flow of the solicitation process.

A good solicitation call is an outcome of intense preparation, cultivation, planning, testing, and research.

On the timeline of development, it is the smallest step. But, on the register of importance, all the other steps can be meaningless without it.

A sage once said there are four things you must do to be successful in any endeavor: plan, plan, plan, and do. Of course, you can over-plan and miss the opportunity to ask at the right time - but most problems in solicitations come from lack of planning, not too much planning!

Be ready ... for the unexpected.

It's one thing to be prepared for a meeting you've arranged and over which you feel you have control. It's quite another to be prepared for the unexpected.

Once, in a brand-new job for a university in the middle of a capital campaign, I had spent several of my first days on the road making calls with the chair of alumni major gifts.

As we were winding down our travels, preparing our contact reports in my office, I had a call from the vice president inquiring about the status of a match we were trying to raise for an NEH challenge. I reported that we were about $65,000 short, but I had some prospects in mind.

When I got off the phone, the volunteer asked me about the challenge. He then revealed that he'd never been asked for his gift and that, although he and his wife had thought of giving $50,000 he would like to close the NEH challenge with a gift of

$65,000.

Was I prepared? No. Did I do what I had [...] the lessons great? You bet.

In another situation, I had carefully plan[ned] [...] call, worked out an elaborate choreography [...] ask, and concerned myself with the other de[...] volunteer worries about when imagining hov[...] go.

Another volunteer and I waited for the pr[...] last-minute strategies. But the prospect had a[...] mind. He walked in, sat down, and said, "Okay, how much do you want?"

We sputtered and tried to delay the answer, but he was insistent. Knowing the importance of a donor-centered meeting, we told him. He smiled and said, "Now, tell me what you were going to tell me. I'm not a good listener when I don't know what the question is going to be!"

In both cases, a gift was made - but the biggest gift was an insight into the importance of being prepared for the unexpected!

Be informed.

For the dynamics of the call to be sturdy yet resilient, you must be as informed as possible about your organization, the project, the prospect, the way in which a gift can be made, and what the recognition can be for the donor. You must also be up to date on any changing circumstances involving the prospect or the organization.

You don't often get a second chance to re-initiate the ask. You may come back to discuss the request, you may bring more information, but that kind of follow up is the natural outcome of a well-structured call.

However, if the call goes badly there's little opportunity to fix it. Most calls that go awry do so because the solicitors haven't done their homework, are unable to answer tough questions or handle objections, make an inappropriate ask, or fail to be donor-focused in the conversation.

Be confident.

There's no substitute for confidence when making sure the dynamics of the solicitation call are successful. There are several aspects to this confidence.

First, have confidence in yourself as a representative of the organization and its mission. Get trained, even if you feel you know how to solicit a prospect; this will reinforce what you already know and further boost your confidence. Practice using the language of the solicitation. And always go in pairs — you will build each other's confidence.

Second, have confidence in your organization. If you're not a believer, how will you convey the importance of investing to another? Be familiar with its strengths, and willing to discuss its shortcomings. There's no need to be defensive. No organization is perfect, and the willingness to discuss strategies for helping the organization shows you are an informed volunteer.

Third, have confidence in the nonprofit sector as the vehicle through which donors build their communities. Speak confidently of the impact an individual's gift will have not just on the organization, but on the overall betterment of the community (seniors helped, teens counseled, animals protected).

Position your organization as part of an overall effort to provide resources and solutions for the community.

Be enthusiastic.

Nothing is as off-putting to the person you're meeting with as the lack of enthusiasm on the part of those who are asking.

Enthusiasm doesn't have to be boisterous or inappropriate: it can be quiet, constant, and signaled by the twinkle in your eye when you speak about the impact of your organization in the community, or by the catch in your voice when you tell the story of one life that was changed by your programs.

Years ago, sales people for CUTCO Cutlery would make door-to-door calls to sell their top-of-the-line knives. When the sales people were trained, and given their satchels of knives to sell, the sales trainer would ask them, "What sells CUTCO?"

And they would have to answer, in unison and in very large voices, "Enthusiasm!" It is the same with us. If we are enthusiastic, others will be. Enthusiasm signals an underlying passion. It is this passion we want to transfer to those who become our donor-investors.

Be yourself.

Among the factors that influence a person's willingness to give is the perception they have of the sincerity and naturalness of the person calling upon them. People don't respond as well to people who are too slick.

While being prepared is essential, and being ready for the unexpected is important, part of the successful dynamic of a solicitation call is that you are yourself.

A story I often tell in my workshops is about a young Stanford volunteer who was assigned to call on an older person with seniority in her company.

She was reluctant to make the call, although she had done a good job getting to know the individual and building a relationship. But finally we reached the point where the call had to be made.

While she hadn't made a gift of the size she was asking, she had made a significant "stretch" gift relative to her own capacity - she was what is called a "proportionate" asker. She was going to ask him to stretch as well.

At the moment of the ask, the woman froze slightly and blurted out the amount of the ask. The prospect looked at her in stunned silence. Then he said, "I've never been asked for a gift that large before!"

And she, without thinking, responded, "Well, I've never ASKED for a gift that large before!" They had a good laugh. The tension was broken. She was herself, and he made the gift.

Remember that the solicitation call is really a conversation. It's an easier conversation if there are three people instead of just one-on-one. But, regardless, be natural, be yourself. It is an essential dynamic of the solicitation call.

Be clear.

In everything you say or show to the prospect, be clear about what you want.

At the outset, use open ended questions to engage the person in conversation that reveals their thinking. But, beyond that, respect the time you have requested (30 minutes at the maximum) and make sure you clearly state what it is you want the prospect to do for your organization and for the community.

Among the specifics you'll want to include in your conversation:

- The amount of the gift you want the person to consider;
- The area within the organization to which the gift may be designated;
- How the gift can be made;
- The impact the gift will have;
- The ways in which the person will be recognized if recogni-

tion is desired;

- The timing of the gift relative to the annual, capital or endowment campaign; and

- Any role you want the person to play within the organization or the campaign.

You don't have much time for this conversation but, if appropriately sequenced with your relationship-building activities, you really won't need much time. And, if the prospect wants you to stay longer, be prepared to stay.

Be alert.

The best laid plans .... We've all had the experience where something goes wrong.

Good preparation can help remedy problems of our own making – for instance, the failure to present the right giving opportunity, not hearing what the prospect is saying, and the like. But it is just as important to recognize faulty dynamics that happen for reasons beyond our control.

People are reluctant to reschedule appointments, and often agree to keep an arranged meeting even when the timing is terrible. Watch for actions that indicate a lack of focus by the prospect: continuing to take phone calls, allowing interruptions from co-workers, unsubtle glances at her watch or the clock, shuffling of unrelated papers on the desk.

If this pattern persists, suggest that perhaps this isn't a good time for the meeting after all, and that you're happy to reschedule.

Often, the person is relieved, will confess to a problem that arose after the meeting was scheduled, and, in the next meeting, will be open, responsive, and grateful.

Be a good closer.

Don't leave anything open, unless the prospect hasn't yet

made a decision. If she needs more time, find out how much. If he needs more information, get the information to him as quickly as possible. If the gift is agreed to in the solicitation call, be sure you have a signed pledge form (if appropriate), or the gift, or have an understood process for how the gift will be made. Never leave behind an unsigned pledge card (you'll lose the reason for returning).

Be sure your agreements are clear. Be enthusiastic and appreciative of the gift (it's all right to be a little noisy now and then), but don't "sell after the close" (that is, make a huge speech about the impact the gift will have in which you basically restate everything you have just spent 30 minutes describing).

Make your exit smooth and gracious, and be sure the person receives a thank you from you with 24 to 48 hours.

Set the machinery in motion for good stewardship, and recognition that is desired by the donor. Most of all, remember that a new relationship has just begun and, rather than the job being over, it is just getting started in a new and better dimension.

●●●

Understanding the dynamics of the solicitation call can introduce an element into the fundraising process that often eludes us: fun. Being part of the transformation of a prospect into a donor-investor requires a thoughtful transaction. These suggestions can help you be successful.

11

THE NEW REALITIES OF CAPITAL CAMPAIGNS

Today's proliferation of capital campaigns is staggering, as communities respond generously and repeatedly to appeals for new buildings, larger program funds, and increased endowment.

If you're thinking of getting on the capital campaign bandwagon, there are some things you should know about the new realities. Times have changed. Wealth has changed. And donors have changed. Most of it is good news, but new strategies and techniques are required.

While many of the old practices (such as cultivation and stewardship) are still important, there are aspects of capital campaigns that must be updated to respond to the changed environment in which communities are raising money.

Here's what you need to know about the new realities of running a capital campaign.

Look beyond the usual prospects to new donor profiles and patterns.

The transfer of wealth in our society, and the generation of new wealth in the 1990s across America from high tech, biotech, and venture capital, added a new and largely unknown layer of potential investors to most communities. Even with the current downsizing of the economy, the residue of the "boom" remains. Large gifts from new sources continue to be made.

And, in geographical communities where this new wealth isn't evident, organizations can more and more look *outside* their communities for those people who share an interest in or passion for the issue their organization is addressing. Many newer donors are more responsive to issues than to particular organizations.

Issues that are broadly attractive to people outside a particular geographic area include the environment, literacy, certain health issues, and other causes of current concern.

In addition to identifying those whose wealth hasn't been previously known, remember that women and previously under-represented racial and ethnic groups are coming strongly into the donor community.

As you survey your potential prospects, think beyond the usual lists. Finding these individuals is a challenge, but Internet access to information – and the filtering of that information by prospect research websites – is moving along very quickly.

Keep in mind, even one new donor from this new area of potential prospects could make the difference in your campaign.

Lead gifts represent a larger percentage of the total campaign.

Capital campaign literature used to advise that the lead gift to a campaign should be at least 10 percent of the total. That percentage has now increased to a minimum of 15 percent and, more likely, 20 percent. The impact of this reality is that organizations need to have the lead donor firmly on board before getting too far along with their campaign planning.

A $25 million campaign to build a new facility for Alzheimer's research and care will require, in some instances, a lead gift of

$5 million. A $200,000 campaign to repair the roof of a community church may require a lead gift of $35,000 or $40,000.

While not true in all campaigns, post-campaign analyses indicate that 90 to 95 percent of funding is coming from 5 to 10 percent of the donors. In one community campaign of $15 million, there were over 2,000 donors but *five* of them gave a total of $7 million (nearly 50 percent of the total).

There are still those organizations that can broker several smaller lead gifts into a pace-setting challenge to others, but the emerging pattern is of one or more very large donors, usually an individual, who "seeds" the campaign.

Donor expectations have changed regarding the "return" on their investment.

While recognition used to be enough (name on a building or classroom, creation of a scholarship fund), now donors are looking for solid evidence of "return."

They want to know the impact their gift is making, how well it is or has been managed or invested, and how their investment in the organization has moved the organization to the next level.

Organizations that undertake capital campaigns must be internally prepared to provide a continuous stream of information and opportunities for their investors to be involved.

Hard hat tours of new buildings, opportunities to meet and interact with scholarship winners, invitations to observe programs or classes are all part of the ongoing stewardship that is required of capital campaign (and all) donors.

Those who give generously to your campaign may expect to sit on your board.

This is not, as many fear, "buying a board seat." This is acknowledging and respecting the desire of a significant donor to monitor, enjoy, and advise on the investment of her gift in the community by getting involved with the organization administering the gift.

We need to remember that people give *through* us, not just *to* us. They're making an investment in their communities, and we're the vehicle they have chosen. Which brings us to the next point.

Competition has never been keener.

In communities across America and overseas, organizations that have never before considered a capital campaign are beginning to feel that now is the time to get underway.

The combination of improved access to wealth, greater maturity of the nonprofit sector, and increasingly well-defined needs of communities, has led to the recognition of this time as a golden era for philanthropy in spite of the decline in overall economic growth.

In defense of feasibility studies (which still have a purpose, even though many donors are reluctant to participate, feeling they are a waste of time), this is one of the reasons to conduct one.

A well-placed question can reveal not only the number of campaigns in the planning phase, but the level to which your prospective donor is already committed to other capital efforts.

Public relations needs have changed.

It's no longer enough to market or promote an organization: new donors and bigger gifts become possible when the marketing focuses on the *issues* the organization is attempting to address.

For example, a campaign for an organization that works with

the aging should focus on the issues inherent in the mission: keeping frail elderly at home, dignity in the aging process, independence and quality of life, the increasingly aged population of America, and how their needs will have an impact on entire communities.

While some donors still respond because of their loyalty to a particular institution, the majority of newer donors are more responsive to issues.

Be sure the case is focused on issues and the desired impact you seek. Public relations and marketing for nonprofits needs to make a sea change in its emphasis.

Campaigns are too time-consuming to be an add-on to a regular staff job.

From the outset, the new realities require dedicated campaign staff. Seed money is increasingly available for building your campaign infrastructure – from foundation management assistance programs or from corporations or individuals who want to see the campaign get underway.

Getting systems in place (computer, communication, cultivation) at the beginning will save a lot of heartache later.

From the beginning, keep the campaign budget separate. This will ensure that campaign costs aren't rolled into your general budget, and allow you to keep track of the true costs of the campaign.

It can also allow you to assign a percentage of regular staffing or other expenses to the campaign, based on their assignment to the special needs the campaign creates.

Create a campaign leadership team that includes, but is not limited to, members of your board.

Face it, your board wasn't recruited to run a capital campaign.

So don't expect them to do it. Expect them to support it financially, and to be the decision-makers for major aspects of the campaign, but identify and recruit a campaign cabinet or steering committee to take on the fundraising and other aspects of the campaign.

Let your board continue to govern, and through the several board members (including the chair of the development committee) who will sit on your campaign cabinet, keep them informed about the campaign.

Set policies at the outset regarding the level to which the cabinet can make campaign-related financial, building, staffing or other decisions, and where the board's review is required.

Acknowledge that you may need to be creative and flexible in soliciting gifts, especially from donors new to philanthropy.

This has several aspects. First, because donors seek organizations whose issues are important to them (in fact, many new family foundations prefer to initiate the approach) they're more ready to give at the beginning of the relationship than traditional donors. In some instances, the gift has already been decided when the contact is made.

This bold paradigm shift has changed research and cultivation dramatically. And, it has put a large burden on the importance of consistent marketing of issues in the community.

Only by marketing in this way can organizations attract the attention of those who can make investments but don't want to be contacted. These people don't need a long cultivation period, but they will expect stewardship and results. Put the energy into the follow up, not to the lead in. That's the first big change.

The second shift may come in the terms of the gift. Savvy

donors may be reluctant to hand over their well-managed investments to organizations whose investment policies or practices may be unknown or unproven.

With these investors, you may need to work out an irrevocable pledge agreement that allows them to retain and invest the gift until you actually need it. This gives the donor confidence that he can keep investing the money, but assures the organization that the money will be there when it is needed.

Prospect to donor ratios are changing.

Often, the go-ahead for a campaign is predicated on the confirmation -- during the planning or feasibility stage -- of the significant lead gift. In campaigns of the past, organizations needed a great number of prospects at the top of the pyramid for the large gifts, and a decreasing number as the gifts got smaller.

As the process of campaigning has gotten more transparent, we're able to identify the top donors earlier and more accurately. The toughest challenge is the need for donors in the middle of the pyramid.

Donor pyramids these days look more like hourglasses: the higher percentages represented by a few top gifts has not cut off the flood of smaller gifts as a campaign rolls to completion. Where the changes have been felt is in the middle band.

Most campaigns find themselves very short of prospects who will give major or special gifts, even if they're successful at finding the large transformational gifts.

The antidote for this is to spend more time cultivating these people before the campaign starts, and to make sure they appreciate the importance of their investment.

•••

Philanthropy has changed. These suggestions can help you be more successful as you plan and implement your next capital campaign.

12

RECRUITING AND RETAINING A CAPITAL CAMPAIGN COMMITTEE

A major factor in organizing and running a successful capital campaign is the quality of the campaign's volunteer leadership. While the board retains final responsibility for the oversight of the drive, the recruitment and retention of dedicated chairs and a strong and capable committee are essential.

There are two different kinds of general volunteer committees for capital campaigns: honorary and active. One is more window dressing, the other is the working committee. A two-tiered structure is quite common.

The honorary committee comprises those individuals in the community who represent power, wealth, and long term connection with the organization. They are the people who lead others to think well of your organization and its importance to the community.

But the real work of the campaign belongs to the active or working campaign chairs (usually two or more; sometimes one) and their committee. This committee, upon whose shoulders the primary responsibilities fall, may be called a campaign steering committee, cabinet, or council. Regardless of their name, these are the critical people without whom your campaign is likely to fail.

Here's what you should know about recruiting and retaining active campaign chairs and a motivated steering committee.

Choose the chair carefully.

Your first step, when searching for the chair, is to identify a pool of candidates for whom your campaign can become their top community priority for the next two to five years. This may in fact be the most important factor in making the initial candidate list. If the leader lacks time, the job will fall back entirely on staff and the campaign will be a difficult experience.

Next, examine the candidates (typically they'll be drawn from board members, former board members, advocates in the community, and major donors).

• Are they committed to your mission and enthusiastic about your organization?

• If not already on the board, can they sit on the board for the duration of the campaign (ex officio or as regular members)?

• Are they individuals who inspire confidence?

• Do they bring out leadership skills in others?

• Can they run a good meeting?

• Are they resilient, flexible, able to work with staff and other volunteers?

• Do they have a network they're willing to draw on to develop the prospect and volunteer base for the campaign?

• Do they want to be deeply involved with the campaign and your organization for the next several years?

Interview those on your list who match the criteria. Let them know how important this campaign is. Don't minimize the time it will take. Instead, let them know how much you believe they are capable of guiding this ambitious project to success. Invest them with your confidence, but also with the reality of the job.

If you have several co-chairs, one must be the "first among equals," responsible for convening meetings, sitting on the board, and being the point person for staff. That individual must be well qualified in all or nearly all of the above areas. The other co-chair(s) may represent a particular constituency, or balance the lead chair in such factors as gender, geography, and age.

Recruit members of the steering committee both for their connection to important constituencies and for their skills in the various functional areas of the campaign.

Segment your important constituencies and identify the skills and experience you'll need (major gifts, planned gifts, endowment management) to tap into each specific group. Then, identify potential committee members who would be able to chair a committee of additional volunteers focused on that constituency.

In a campaign for a building project for an Episcopal cathedral, the chairs recruited representatives from the diocese, deaneries, and parishes, as well as those skilled in architecture, construction, major gifts, media, special events, planned gifts, and public relations.

Create job descriptions for both the chair(s) and the committee.

A job description serves as both a recruitment and a management tool. Setting standards at the outset will save heartache later.

If someone is too busy to do the job, don't recruit her. While the name may be important to the committee, if it's only a name little will be accomplished. Appoint those who can serve in name only to the honorary committee instead.

The board chair should recruit the campaign chair(s), using a copy of the job description, and it should be discussed and agreed to.

An important responsibility of chairs and committee members is early financial support of the campaign, at a level that represents a stretch. They must also make calls on others to solicit their support. Be as specific as possible about what is expected.

Discuss the job descriptions with the candidate to make sure the expectations are understood.

Set a meeting calendar for the year and stick to it.

Busy people like to set dates on their calendars well in advance. They don't like it when those dates get changed. Choose the second Tuesday or third Friday at 8 a.m. or noon or whatever works for your committee. Meet monthly throughout the campaign, taking August and December off if you can.

Sub-committee meetings should also be scheduled for a year at a time, if possible. At times, these committees (e.g., building or endowment) may need to meet more or less often.

It's better to schedule a meeting and cancel it, than to try to schedule a meeting on short notice with busy people. Stick to the calendar, and, when there are reasons to move a date that has been long-set, explain the reasons and apologize for the inconvenience.

Get the chair(s) and committee campaign gift commitments before you ask them to ask others.

In a campaign, it's essential to solicit the board first, and then to involve the board chair in soliciting the campaign steering committee chairs. The chairs then enlist and solicit their committee; those committee members in turn solicit their committee members.

Every ask that's made of a campaign leader (including all committee members) should be done in person, even if the stretch gift involved is not a "major" gift to your campaign. All leadership volunteers should be treated as major donors because of their time commitment, giving and advocacy roles.

Give assignments to all members (no free rides).

On a steering committee, all members should have committee and solicitation assignments. If a member does not, for example, have time to chair the major gifts committee, he should at least serve on the committee. It creates resentment among hardworking committee members to see that some members are participating in strategic decisions that they are not helping to carry out.

Keep meetings focused on both the mechanics and the impact of the campaign.

Just as all board meetings should have a "product demonstration" to keep the passion and involvement fresh, so should campaign steering committee meetings. Be sure each meeting features a short presentation by a client, program staff person, community member, or other person who's familiar with the program and can inspire the committee as to how the results of the campaign will make an impact on the community. This will keep the engines humming.

Otherwise, the "mechanics" of the campaign (list review, problems with construction, delays in pledge fulfillment) can diminish the energy of committee members and potentially dampen their enthusiasm for asking.

If enthusiasm lags, determine the reason and fix the problem -- or de-enlist.

If a committee member begins to slip in his responsibilities, address the situation immediately. Have the chair of the steering committee call and find out why.

If the problem can be fixed (poor communications from staff, unhappy about a lack of support from her volunteers), devise strategies to fix it. If it cannot be fixed (new job, new baby, moving, no longer interested in the organization, irreparable personality conflict with a staff or volunteer leader), then the steering committee chair should de-enlist the committee member and thank him for his service. Perhaps there's a way to involve that individual on the honorary committee or in an ad hoc way.

The same process should be applied by subcommittee chairs to their members. A non-performing volunteer is signaling for help: find out what the person needs to do the job, or if the person would rather not continue. This need not be a bitter or unhappy transaction. Keep the conversation focused on how the person has helped, whether they see a continuing role for themselves, and if not, if they have ideas about other leaders who might take their place.

Be sure the committee's relationship to the board is clear and observed (the board is not off the hook just because there is a campaign committee).

The board has ultimate responsibility for the success of the campaign. The campaign chairs are recruited by the board chair, and one of the chairs should sit on the board either as a member or ex officio for the duration of the campaign.

Board members should serve on campaign subcommittees, and are expected to make solicitations. The fact that there's a steering committee doesn't reduce the board's responsibility. It just shifts the authority for ongoing campaign business to a board-appointed committee that duly reports to the board at every meeting. The steering committee is accountable to the board.

Celebrate them at every opportunity.

If you want to keep the chairs and committee motivated, celebrate them often. Stay informed about the progress of their calls, and reinforce their success and their efforts (even if unsuccessful).

Think of ways to provide incentives for completing the calls (one organization gave a "You've Earned Your Spurs" certificate for volunteers after they made their first solicitation). It "spurred" others to make theirs!

Start each steering committee meeting with an "SOS" — Share Our Success — session. It is a wonderful way to celebrate.

One steering committee chair brought a box of Kudo candy bars to each meeting, and would give "kudos" to those who had made a difficult call, completed a difficult negotiation, or in other ways pursued their leadership responsibilities.

We tend to think of the big celebration at the end of a campaign: that will come sooner, and with a much more loyal and renewed group of volunteers, if they are celebrated all along the way.

•••

Campaign success is measured in several ways: dollars raised, donors increased, visibility enhanced, and volunteer leadership growth. Creating and retaining strong volunteer leadership committees will help you accomplish all of those goals.

13

CONDUCTING A CAMPAIGN FEASIBILITY STUDY

The debate about feasibility studies for capital or endowment campaigns goes on.

Some organizations shun them and still conduct successful campaigns; others that forego a study struggle and fail for lack of appropriate information.

To be sure, a feasibility study can be costly ($25,000 and up). But if the study is good, it can be worth it. From a good study, your organization will learn how it's perceived in the marketplace, which aspects of your cause or project to emphasize in your case statement, and potential objections which can be addressed in materials and meetings.

Further, individuals interested in leadership roles will be identified, you'll hear confidential feedback about the history or operations of your organization and, most importantly, you'll be able to gauge the inclination of individual and institutional funders to give to the campaign.

The following suggestions are offered for those who are still debating the options or for those organizations that have decided to conduct a study.

Don't do it yourself

Tempting as it is to save money and time, it's not an objective study if someone "in house" does it. Why? Two principal reasons: people won't be as candid with someone who is on staff; and staff people have a hard time staying objective in their questions and responses.

Also, a good feasibility study will assess both internal and external readiness for a campaign. An objective internal study simply cannot be done by someone who is on staff.

Be sure you have good chemistry with the consultant you do choose, and that you're confident of his intelligence and ability to market your organization.

The need for good chemistry is true with any consultant you choose, but particularly for a feasibility study. Things have a way of getting delayed with a study (canceled appointments, changes in meeting places, appointments that take longer than expected to set up) and there's a big need to work closely through some logistical minefields with your consultant.

If you find you're annoyed with the consultant's approach or style, cut your losses during the planning stage. It's better to lose a few weeks than try to work with someone you don't feel good about.

In choosing a consultant, it's also critical to choose someone in whose intelligence and ability to market your organization you have the utmost confidence. This individual (and his associates — be sure to meet them, too) is going to be the first contact with your potential funders. Be sure the person can master the information he will need to know, and that his style and personality will convey the integrity of the project or organization.

Require quantitative as well as qualitative questions on the

structured questionnaire.

Statements in feasibility study reports like, "Most of the participants in the study supported the idea" or "Many felt this was not a good idea" won't satisfy the needs of left-brain (and most right-brain) board members who need to make a tough decision about a campaign.

Be sure the consultant is including scaled, weighted, and ranking questions to balance and verify the narrative questions. Then you will have report findings that read, "Average assessment of the visibility of the organization was 2.2 on a scale of 4" or "The various campaign priorities were tested by asking the participants to rank them. In order of their ranking, the priorities selected were .... "

Ask to see a previous report prepared by the consultant.

Reports can range from 10 pages to 60 pages, be organized or random, specific or vague, include next steps or stop with the study's findings. Be sure to review a report before signing a contract. Also, be very specific about what kind of report you want. Some organizations don't want a lot of paper; others won't feel they've gotten their money's worth unless they have a bound, thick study.

Be specific about what you want from the consultant.

Communicated expectations are the foundation of a successful consultant-client relationship. Be specific in your Request for Proposals (RFP), and repeat those expectations in your interviews and in the final contract. Let the consultant know the maximum timeframe (understanding that delays can occur that are no fault of anyone's), what internal and external issues should be covered in the study, the format you would like for the report, and your understanding of the fee and payment structure. Have a signed agreement with a mutual termination clause if the study needs to be stopped for any reason.

Work closely with the consultant at the outset of the study, to ensure that the right people are interviewed and that the consultant has the support he needs.

While the consultant should review the various segments of the constituencies to be included (business, social, educational leaders) and also provide the draft letter of invitation, the actual names must be generated in most cases by the organization. Of course, if the consultant is from the community, he can be helpful in providing contact information.

Have a point person on staff to respond to the consultant once the study begins. If the organization is setting up the appointments, communicate the schedule to the consultant in a timely way. If the consultant is setting the appointments, be sure the lists are accurate and that you've provided the consultant with a signed copy of each letter sent, on letterhead. In that way, if the consultant has to fax a second copy of the letter, he will have one that is signed and addressed to that interviewee.

Choose the signer of the letter of invitation carefully.

Many studies have fallen far short of their required interviewees because the wrong person signed the letter. Choose someone with visibility, connection with the community and the organization, and someone well-respected.

In one study for a community cultural center, the mayor of the community signed the letter. There was nearly 90 percent participation by those on the interview list. In another study, a controversial executive director became impatient and signed the letter rather than wait for the signature of the community leader who had been identified. The result: just 35 percent of those contacted agreed to participate.

Don't ask for results before the study is done.

It's not over until the last interview. Interim reports shouldn't be required (though you'll want progress updates on the number of interviews completed, how many still pending, how many refused). If something comes up during the study which is important for the client to know (for example, a foundation has said it will provide start up funds if the request is made within 10 days), then the consultant will convey that information. Otherwise, sit tight and wait for the full report.

Require a verbal as well as a written presentation.

It's not enough to submit a written report. Your board should hear the results, and the consultant will want to present them. This is a major investment of time and money, and maximum board attendance should be encouraged. Provide an overhead or PowerPoint projector and ask the consultant to put the key points into graph form (this is where quantitative questions can really tell a story).

Whatever the outcome -- do it, delay it, forget it -- extract from the process those things which will benefit the organization in the long run.

Even in studies which say delay it or forget it, the recommendations should provide a checklist and game plan for bringing the organization into a position where a capital or endowment campaign *is* feasible.

The exercise is seldom in vain. Information about ways in

which internal structure and external relations can be improved can help the organization position itself in a stronger way. In one "delay it" study for an organization, the recommendations were sequential and comprehensive, enabling the executive director to use the recommendations as a plan for the next two years — checking off each recommendation as it was accomplished. At the end, they started the campaign. And, it succeeded.

•••

The benefits of conducting an objective feasibility study are many, and the majority of organizations conduct them before undertaking a capital campaign. However, each organization is different and some campaigns succeed well without a study.

If you know your donor-investors well, and you have lots of them, you may decide to forego the study. If you *do* conduct a study, these points will help with your strategy.

14

TRANSFORMATIONAL GIFTS

More and more, they are front-page news. Even in a time of diminished wealth and a level of "psychic poverty," large gifts are still being made.

Gordon Moore, founder of Intel, gave $650 million to Cal Tech. The University of Colorado received $250 million to establish The Coleman Institute.

In the late 1990s, we saw these gifts:

A $150 million gift to Stanford University from entrepreneur Jim Clark, a former Stanford professor and founder of several high tech companies (Silicon Graphics, Netscape, and others) to fund a multi-disciplinary biomedical engineering initiative.

A $12 million gift to the College of the Ozarks from the estate of Dr. Joe T. McKibben, a non-alum retired physician, for scholarships and a new academic center.

A $5 million gift to the George Washington University School of Medicine from Laszlo Tauber, restricted to scholarships for descendents of World War II veterans.

A $3 million gift from the Wolf family of Denver and Houston to construct a building at the University of Colorado Boulder School of Law.

A $250,000 gift to the Boys and Girls Clubs of Alamosa, Colorado, from the El Pomar Foundation of Colorado Springs to construct a club house.

These gifts — some huge, others modest only by comparison — have a common tie: their impact. Because of their size, relative to the overall budget of the organization or the project, they are *transformational*.

Transformational gifts may be categorized as "big" or "major" gifts, but what distinguishes them is their unique capacity to alter the programs, perception, and future of an organization. More than gifts, they are true investments in the future of an organization and of the community.

Drawn from several years of research and thinking, recently accelerated by the ever-increasing number of these gifts, here's what you should know about transformational giving and how to position your organization to attract such gifts.

Many of these gifts are from the "new" philanthropists.

Responsible for many of these transformational gifts are: the cyber and venture capital rich; women; ethnic and racial groups previously under-represented in philanthropy; and those who have become wealthy through the intergenerational transfer of several trillions of dollars currently underway in America.

The old methods for identifying, cultivating and even soliciting don't always work. Many of the new philanthropists are inexperienced donors, and don't show up on the usual lists. Further, they often seek out organizations and don't want organizations to seek them. For those who research and track potential donors, the challenges are great -- but so are the opportunities.

Many of the individuals capable of transformational gifts have formed philanthropic organizations on their own: donor-advised funds within their venture capital or financial firms, independent family foundations or donor-advised funds located in and managed by community foundations (at the Community Foundation Silicon Valley, many such funds have been established).

In several communities (Seattle, Silicon Valley), "social venture" organizations have been created by newly wealthy younger people -- organizations where the focus is not just the giving of money, but also getting involved in community projects.

This isn't your father's philanthropy -- it is more like your mother's.

An interesting phenomenon of transformational giving -- especially from younger donors — is that it patterns the outcomes of the studies done in women's philanthropy at the University of Wisconsin and UCLA. A key discovery was that women tended to get involved first, then make a financial commitment.

Traditional male donors, on the other hand, would often make a gift first (particularly when asked by a peer) and then (perhaps) get involved on the board later.

New philanthropists -- particularly those making transformational gifts -- want to get involved with both the definition of the gift and the institution it will transform.

The gift to Stanford from Jim Clark was the result of three years of conversation, visioning, exploration, communication (much of it by e-mail) and program definition. And, Clark's involvement as a former professor was coupled with his gratitude for the opportunities Stanford had provided him to develop the research that led to the founding of his successful companies.

In another case, several of the transformational donors to Sage Hill, an independent high school in Orange County, California, are intensely involved with numerous aspects of the school's curricular and physical plant development.

The engagement of these individuals in organizations and institutions is of mutual benefit.

Transformational donors invest in issues and ideas -- not just in institutions.

Interviewed in an annual report of the Community Foundation Silicon Valley several years ago, one young couple, Ray and Joanne Lin, put it this way, "We fund change, not charity."

Another philanthropist, a young woman who has established her own foundation, commented in response to a question regarding the kinds of organizations she funds, "I don't fund organizations, I fund issues."

While traditional "community philanthropy" — the funding of the basic arts, health, education and other institutions that comprise most communities — is still very important to experienced philanthropists and many new donors, there is this trend towards looking for the organizations that address issues (children, homelessness, poverty, domestic violence, substance abuse) and funding them not because the organization is familiar to the donor, but because the issue is important.

This shift puts a new emphasis in the marketing thrust for nonprofits: the focus has to be on the mission (the need that's being met) and the values implicit in that mission.

Too often, mission statements and marketing pieces focus too much on the organization, and not on its values and results. More than 10 years ago, in an article in the Wall Street Journal, Peter Drucker commented, "People no longer give to charity, they buy into results." As usual, Mr. Drucker was ahead of his time.

Transformational giving, because it transforms organizations, will often attract funding for both infrastructure and programming.

Capacity-building grants are becoming more common. Community and other foundations have been providing "technical" or "management assistance" for years: salary support, computer funding, and the like. Now, however, individual and family foundation funders are also investing in stability.

They are making these commitments because the issue is so important, they're willing to invest in making sure the organization has the internal systems to support continued fulfillment of its mission.

In one such instance, an organization with strong mental health programs highly dependent on government funding was given both a program grant and an organizational assistance grant by a family foundation.

The rationale was made clear in the grant: the mission of the organization was important to the funder; the dependency on government funding was a concern to them; the creation of a separate foundation to raise and manage private funding was essential to the future health of the organization; and current staffing needed assistance to create that foundation and get the fundraising started.

Thus funding was given not only for programming but to provide counsel and coaching to the high-potential person already on staff to develop him for the job.

Transformational donors have some exciting characteristics -- ones that are changing the face of philanthropy as well as the institutions and communities in which they have invested.

These are the principal characteristics that emerged in the research, observations and interviews conducted for my book, *High Impact Philanthropy*, co-authored with Alan Wendroff in 2000:

• Transformational donors invest in results and in the values implicit in those results;

• They seek values-driven organizations, often without realizing that it is the values that are attracting them;

• They want organizations to accept their ideas and opinions, not just their money;

• They're impatient for results - and sometimes for the ask;

• They're willing to make longer term investments;

• They want to transform institutions and society;

• They often want a base of power in the program or organization.

These attributes in some cases represent a confirmation of more traditional philanthropy, but there are several that have broad implications for the way nonprofits must re-tool some of their approaches. The next several points will deal with these implications.

If your organization wants to attract a transformational gift, it must focus on results, not needs.

An article by Scott Kirsner entitled, "Nonprofit Motive," in the September, 1999 issue of Wired, had this subtitle: "The new breed of Silicon Valley philanthropists would make Mother Teresa crunch the numbers. Call it virtue capital."

In the article Kirsner highlighted the philanthropic leadership of Steve Kirsch, founder of Infoseek. Kirsch, according to the article, "likes groups that are ambitious, he wants his money to make a measurable difference, and he prefers that the altruism be balanced by sound business sense. He likes being intellectually stimulated by what he underwrites."

Later, the article says: "... the new breed of high tech philanthropists want to reinvent the art of generosity. They share

(Kirsch's) sense that simply giving money away is too passive and uninvolved. They want to lend business expertise, identify and support 'social entrepreneurs' hungry to shake up the non-profit world, and quantify their results. In short, they want to create a new kind of charity. But they don't call it that. They call it venture philanthropy."

Our sector has two bottom lines: financial and values. We must show results in both. For the financial we provide numbers; whereas, the values are shown in both statistics (how many are helped, how many lives are enhanced) *and* stories (about the real people behind the statistics).

In the same article, Vanessa Kirsch (no relation to Steve) who founded New Profit, a Boston-based venture philanthropy group, said, "Traditional philanthropy isn't based on performance and results."

Whether or not that is true, that's the perception out there. And organizations must position themselves in new ways to appear results-oriented.

Even though the technology bubble has burst, the interest of those made wealthy in its boom years is still strong. And so are their expectations of our sector.

If your organization wants to attract a transformational gift, it must also focus on the issues, ideas, and values inherent in the mission.

Often this starts with reevaluating the mission statement. Is it so corporate that it only conveys what your organization does, and not why you do it? If so, chances are it doesn't convey your values.

We function in a message-driven society — so much so that it takes up to seven exposures to a message before it can break through the resistance we've developed.

But, advertisers who seek consumers for the purpose of having them spend thousands of dollars on cars, high tech communications devices, and other such indulgences, aren't shy about talking about values long before they mention their product.

Not long ago, an advertising insert in several magazines with affluent readership had the following text:

"We build walls. With our everyday routines. And our cram-it-all-in schedules. Walls that make a nasty habit of separating us from our dreams. But, what if there were no walls? What if there were a way to break straight through to your dreams? There is. All you need is an outfitter with the right equipment. Ford is your outfitter. Outfitting you with the most far-reaching sport utility vehicles on earth. Climb in. And watch the walls come tumbling down."

So little mention of the cars; so much emphasis on the values.

And, you needn't have a huge advertising budget to get a message across. Integrate your values even into the smallest unit of your outreach: Stanford University Libraries sent a simple thank you card to its donors.

A sketch of the library was on the front of the fold-over card. Inside, the text read: "Your gift to the Stanford University Libraries helps us assemble the sources, the arguments, the hypotheses, the wisdom and controversies of the ages. For all those here and those yet to come, please accept our gratitude."

It was signed by the University librarian. It doesn't need to be poetry, but it needs to catch people's attention and engage their thinking and involvement.

For Sage Hill School in Orange County, the values of diversity, service learning, excellence, and opportunity to thrive have been the preeminent message in its marketing for enrollment and for the campaign to build the school.

Transformational gifts may be decades in the making, or they may come in more quickly than you can imagine.

A bequest of a million dollars or more for an organization with a modest budget or programming is clearly transformational. Many times, these gifts aren't known until we are notified. They represent decades of involvement or observation by the donor, and a decision to make a lasting investment in an organization.

These kinds of gifts are more the product of faith in an organization's ability to continue operating and acting long after a person has died.

Contrast that kind of gift with some of the transformational gifts that have been received. Sometimes, they are surprises, too. But, because they are issues-focused, or about change, they have an urgency about them. The urgency is based not on the organization's perceived need for money, but on the donor's perception of the urgency of the need.

An endowment campaign feasibility study for a 4-H after-school activity program in public housing projects in Oakland, California, yielded many funders interested in making a gift to the program -- but not for endowment.

The problem 4-H is working to ameliorate was felt to be "too urgent" for an endowment approach. Instead, corporations, foundations, and individuals were willing to consider six-figure gifts that would more immediately transform the programming for these at-risk children.

And, while solicitation of transformational gifts should be done through personal conversations and meetings, the supporting dialog will often be done on the Internet. These are, in many cases, very busy people. The process is donor-centered, of course, and that includes adapting your systems to their needs.

Other characteristics of transformational givers provide additional reasons for looking carefully at your cultivation, solicitation, and stewardship systems.

Even more traditional donors who decide to make a transformational gift are increasingly impatient with the pace of the nonprofit sector and the bureaucracy of some institutions. And, younger donors are very impatient, particularly those who have worked in high-tech fast-paced start-ups.

When they want information, they want it by return e-mail or phone call. The process inherent in so much of what nonprofits have traditionally done in donor development may have to be accelerated.

Internalize the steps and skip past those that don't seem necessary. And, if suggestions are made about speeding up processes or stripping out a few layers of bureaucracy, listen to these advisors. They've known success either because of their creation of wealth, their emergence into mainstream philanthropy, their climb up the corporate ladder, or their management of inherited wealth and their redirection of it into social ventures.

They are looking to make long-term investments — many are using the venture capital model of a minimum five-year investment — but they want short-term results and a non-bureaucratic environment in which to be engaged and savor the impact of their giving.

If you remember four "I" words, you will be better positioned to engage a potential transformational donor.

Focus on Issues, offer opportunities for Involvement, remember that this gift is truly an Investment, and remember to focus on and convey the Impact to the donor-investor and to the community.

•••

These suggestions should give you food for thought and a platform for action. In communities around America (and increasingly, other parts of the world) there are individuals and foundations with wealth that they wish to invest in their communities. Position your organization to be an agent for their dreams.

15

PLANNING AND IMPLEMENTING A YEAR-END FUND-RAISING PROGRAM

There are two "year ends" for most nonprofits: fiscal and calendar. We raise money during both. The former is due to our need to close the year well. The latter is done to let donors give during the most common time of sharing in our country -- November and December.

So whether your fiscal year is just underway, half-over, or coincides with the end of the calendar-year, it always seems to spring upon us fast. And almost anytime is a good time to begin planning your year-end appeals.

It's tempting to do the same things you've always done, particularly if they seem successful.

But it may be time to take a fresh look at your practices; to retain your successful messages and practices but to develop a new plan based on discussions with your donors, volunteers, and staff.

Here are the most important things to know about putting your year-end campaign on a more innovative, inclusive, and successful footing.

Take time to analyze last year's successes and failures.

Be willing to take a hard look at last year's campaign before you start this year's. Figure out what worked, and be willing to admit what didn't work.

If you had one volunteer in personal solicitation who, quite frankly, made most of the asks, that's an area you need to work on.

If your donor acquisition mailing lost money for the third year in a row, analyze why. Look at the lists you're using. Talk with your mail house.

If your renewals are down, analyze your message. Maybe your letters have a dunning tone, rather than one that invites investment. Or perhaps they focus on your institutional needs, rather than on your results.

Do both a financial and a message/impact analysis. If you have a large donor base, and are concerned about your results, do a donor focus group. Find out what motivates them, and build those ideas into your appeals.

Take time to develop a year-end plan with goals, objectives, and action steps.

When you finish your analysis, develop a solid year-end plan. Too often, for short-term funding efforts, organizations set aside the formal planning process and "just do it."

But a plan provides internal guideposts that keep any initiative on track, and a plan also gives volunteers a sense of the importance of the year-end campaign and of their involvement.

Cover all the strategies you'll use: mail, phone, personal solicitation. Cover all constituencies: individuals, corporations, and small family or private foundations.

It doesn't have to be an elaborate plan, but it should have

dollar, donor, and other goals; measurable objectives; and an easily understood action plan that boils each task down to who will do it, what resources are needed, and the date by which it needs to be done. Attach a list of staff and volunteers who are involved with the campaign and include current phone numbers.

This becomes the "battle plan" for the duration of the campaign, and is a document that indicates both the professionalism of the organization and the importance you place on clear communications. At the end of the year-end campaign, it is the basis on which you'll do the planning analysis for the remainder of your fiscal-year fundraising or for the next year.

Keep the format simple, and use the plan at all status meetings with staff and volunteers.

Crown that plan with one innovative strategy that will energize the plan and your organization.

For one organization, it was the introduction of Thankathons as follow up to the year-end campaign. For another, it was the first-time development of personal solicitation teams. For yet another, it was bringing in an outside trainer to provide coaching for personal solicitation volunteers and staff.

Other innovations might be a mini-retreat for all campaign volunteers to review the plan; recruitment of a "creative team" to review themes and messages before the campaign is launched; sending a bookmark instead of a brochure with the direct mail letters; having a "PS-athon" so board members and other volunteers can come for an afternoon or evening and add personal notes to letters that will go out first class.

Your innovation should emerge from your analysis, and be incorporated into your plan.

Recruit a team of volunteers that represents a good mixture

of ideas, energy, experience, and vision.

Veterans of your year-end campaigns — whether board members, former board members, development committee members, or community members who work with you on an ad hoc basis — will learn from and be inspired by new faces and ideas around the planning table.

The year-end campaign committee should represent the various constituencies (individuals, corporations, foundations) and strategies (personal solicitation, mail acquisition, mail/phone renewals).

Recruit a chair who has experience, but not someone who's resistant to new ideas and new people. The chair works with staff to identify volunteers for this steering committee, and should take the leadership role in enlistment. If that's not possible, staff should go ahead and do it.

Provide an initial meeting where they can stir their ideas around, respond to the plan, and make commitments to uphold their part of the campaign. Have a mid-point meeting to check progress, and a post-campaign meeting to review results. In between, various subcommittees (mail, phone, corporate) can meet. Meetings, however, are much less important than getting the job done.

Assign volunteers to areas where they will flourish.

Whether they are new to your campaign or veterans, chat with all of those you are enlisting for the campaign and find out what motivates them. Just because someone has always had a particular role in your campaign doesn't mean that's the role she wants to continue. It's important to know what people will and will not do.

Many people are very uncomfortable making face-to-face solicitations, but are confident making phone solicitations. Others despise the phone, and prefer to write or sign letters. Still others know that face-to-face is the only kind of solicitation that really builds relationships.

By determining their talents and comfort zone before assigning them, you can avoid having to hover, cajole or de-enlist.

Provide volunteers with training and coaching.

A training session is an investment in your volunteers and in the success of the campaign. If your volunteers are training-resistant, call it something else: leadership session, campaign planning, strategy session, kick-off.

The session needs to be upbeat, focused, and geared to your organization's needs and philosophy. Training can be done by an inside staff or board person who's experienced and respected, or by an outside facilitator.

While you cannot enforce a "mandatory" session, it should be one of the items stipulated in the recruitment process. And, even if your volunteers have been engaged in fundraising for years, convey to them that this session will focus on new ideas and approaches; review the goals and deadlines; and is an opportunity for them to be mentors to new volunteers who are joining their ranks. The training session should be done as close as possible to the time the solicitations will be made, so that volunteers remember the critical points.

Coaching, which is done one-on-one, is also a critical aspect of raising the volunteer comfort level. With coaching, the volunteer meets with the staff or volunteer leader and reviews the specific aspects of that individual's solicitation assignments. This is also done as close as possible to the time the solicitations will be made.

Done properly, training and coaching will be seen increasingly by volunteers as a "perk" -- and some of the skills you will convey (listening, questioning, closing) may also be skills your volunteers can apply in their paying jobs.

Be enthusiastic, even if this is the 27th time you've done a year-end campaign and it feels like "same old-same old."

There's nothing more dampening to volunteers and other staff people than cynicism about a campaign, prospects, or the process. Whatever needs to be done to keep the enthusiasm up, do it. If you're feeling cynical, keep it to yourself or set up a hotline with another development officer or executive director and share your gripes with them.

Educate your entire organization (program staff and administration) about the year-end campaign's activities, and how they can be part of the development team.

Another way to maintain your own enthusiasm is to create a true development team-feeling within the organization. Program staff people can be great resources for mailings, personal visits, corporate, or foundation proposals. But if they feel imposed upon or uninvolved, they won't be good team members.

Their perception of development may be based on a belief that it's only about asking for money. They may not see their role as part of the team: providing information, being at the organization for tours or teas, speaking informally or formally in the community on behalf of the organization, or just their daily interaction with clients.

Educate the entire staff about the year-end campaign, how they can help, what it entails, and what the goals are. During the campaign, maintain a posture of professionalism, consistency, commitment, and enthusiasm.

Convey the good news regularly: one organization put out a

"Good Newsletter" every week during their year-end campaign -- a simple single or double-sided desk-top report that was put in everyone's (actual or email) mailbox in the organization. It listed the gifts, the totals, told funny or warm stories about staff and volunteer experiences asking for gifts, and generally conveyed the complexity of the campaign while focusing on results. The support that development received from program and administration increased substantially.

Be sure your donor recognition and stewardship program has been reviewed for its successes and weak points, and that levels and practices are appropriate for your donors.

In your analysis for year-end campaign planning, don't neglect recognition and stewardship.

Look at your recognition levels and verify that they still fit the pattern of giving in your organization. Also, see if people are getting "stuck" at a particular level and consider ways you might encourage them to increase their gifts. Also check your organization's progress with regard to stewardship.

Remember that the true "return" on an investment isn't the mug, the tote bag, the free tickets, but the knowledge that a gift has made an impact in the community. Be careful not to focus entirely on tangible benefits of giving, but to devise recognition and stewardship that will be mission-anchored and reflective of your organization's values.

Stick to your deadlines, and plan small celebrations when each milestone is reached.

When the year is over, the year-end campaign is over. While most organizations keep their books open for a few days into the new year to record gifts that came in during the holidays, the active campaigning is finished.

Remember to celebrate. It is a festive time of year for most people, and these celebrations need not be elaborate. Gauge your celebrations against measurable objectives: dollars raised, contacts made, parts of the campaign completed, an extraordinary gift or experience, and the like.

These can be spontaneous or planned, large or small. They don't even have to be done in groups. A celebration can also be sending flowers to the first volunteer to complete his or her assignments.

A local merchant is often willing to donate dinner for two, tickets to an event or another award that can be given to staff or volunteers who do an outstanding job.

Some organizations regard celebration as an intrinsic part of their culture; others have to be persuaded that the time taken to savor success is important. Whatever it takes to build celebrations into your campaign, do it. They energize and motivate, and the benefits will far outweigh the time they take.

•••

A year-end campaign is vital to the financial success of most nonprofits. By building in these strategies, the campaign can also have great benefits in team-building, perception of professionalism and increased donor, volunteer and staff involvement.

16

STARTING A STEWARDSHIP PROGRAM

Stewardship, the continued involvement, cultivation, and care of those who give to your organization, is the most important practice in the development process.

It is an organization's philosophical commitment to the value and importance of donors as well as their gifts; a belief, an attitude, that each donor — whether individual, corporate, or foundation — contributes more than money, and that gifts are a symbol of the donor's belief in the values, purpose and importance of the organization.

Donors who feel they are valued only for their gifts, or who feel neglected after giving, quickly sour on an organization or even the nonprofit sector as a whole. Donors who are drawn more deeply into a relationship with an organization through effective stewardship become its advocates and promoters.

Imagine the best scenario possible. With your various year-end giving efforts you acquire 100 new donors, renew several hundred more, and upgrade still hundreds of others. What happens after the thank-you letter is sent?

• How are you going to involve those individuals in a way that will let them know you regard their gift as a symbol of their faith and appreciation in your ability to meet a particular need in the community?

• How are you going to let them know during the year that you regard them as partners with you in providing essential services to the community?

• How are you going to let them know that their gift is being used appropriately, and that you regard it as an investment in the community, not just in your organization?

Here's what you should know to get on the right track.

If your board hasn't adopted a policy regarding stewardship, start by creating and approving one.

Many boards don't really understand what stewardship is all about. A policy that implants the importance of donors and stewardship securely into the systems of the organization is good for the board, and good for your donors. This isn't a detailed plan for stewardship; rather, it's a commitment to the philosophy and practice.

By ensuring that a board policy is in place, stewardship is more apt to be a steady practice, rather than an occasional spurt of activity. Once you've done this -- which may require education about stewardship from staff, a board member, or outside facilitator -- then you're ready to get started.

The policy will become part of the culture of your organization if there's a plan to go with it.

Organize a stewardship planning task force involving board members, other volunteers, a development or administrative staff member, and some donors.

Involving donors in such a process is particularly important. They are an excellent resource for setting up a program to maintain donor relationships because they have experience and perspective. Give them a leadership role, and let them be a part of the team that presents the proposed stewardship program plan to the board. That plan should include the following:

• An analysis of the current donor base according to the way gifts cluster.

• The creation of four or five giving (recognition) levels based on where the gifts cluster.

• Naming of the recognition levels. Avoid being too clever or too complex. If possible try to keep the names linked to the mission; otherwise use generic names such as donor, patron, benefactor.

• Determination of the "benefits" for each level. These should be kept very mission-related and should reflect IRS guidelines regarding the value of "givebacks."

• Review and approval by the development committee of these levels and benefits.

• Inclusion of levels and benefits in all fundraising and stewardship materials, including newsletter reports of giving.

• A mechanism for monitoring the relationship between stewardship and recognition.

• An annual evaluation process that reviews the program, benefits and impact of the stewardship program.

Begin involving donors with their first gift.

If you wait until a donor reaches some magical, internally designated threshold of giving before you start practicing thoughtful stewardship, it may be too late. This is why "thankathons" were invented. When groups of volunteers, staff, or program beneficiaries get on the telephone to thank donors (regardless of the size of their gift), good things happen.

Donors hear personally that their gift is appreciated and will be used wisely. Callers have a chance to talk to other donors in the community, and the shared enthusiasm is mutually beneficial. A deepening involvement can occur on both sides of the telephone connection.

Always done in addition to a written letter or receipt, the thankathon is an important aspect of stewardship.

Stewardship becomes evident to donors when you alternate your messages to them.

A trusted rule says that for every one time you ask someone for money you should contact him or her two other times without asking for money. Ask for their opinion. Send out a proposal or brochure draft with "DRAFT" stamped on it. Invite their feedback.

Put together a focus group around a new program initiative or funding possibility. Call them in a thankathon. Invite them to a lecture or presentation. Include them in a no-fee tea or reception to meet a visiting or resident professional.

Send out occasional "white papers" treating an issue that your organization is dealing with locally and relate it to a larger national or international issue by including a thoughtful article or newspaper clipping. Draw the donor's attention to what you're doing locally to address this critical issue, and let them know that their gift helps make that possible.

If you don't allocate money in your budget for stewardship, it won't work.

Make stewardship activities — donor receptions, special mementos for large gift donors, dinner or refreshments for a thankathon — an integral part of your development program budget.

The budget for special fundraising activities or events is always easier to justify than the budget for donor development. Fundraising results are usually immediate and measurable. The impact of donor development groundwork may not be evident for years.

But donor development — and stewardship as a primary function — make fundraising successful. While difficult to measure precisely in its financial return, stewardship affects the entire bottom line: an overall increase in giving and a growth in donor retention will follow if it is done consistently and well.

Implement stewardship practices that are appropriate to the amount of the gift, your budget and your organization's image.

Donors are uneasy when they believe that a memento or event is too expensive or inconsistent with their image of the organization. They wonder if their gift has been squandered.

Scale back the tangible benefits afforded to donors and focus on communicating the real benefits: the impact of the gift on the fulfillment of the mission in the community.

Find out what kind of involvement your major gift and planned gift donors want.

Don't assume that everyone wants to belong to a "giving club." Many don't. They may be very busy with other organizations and their own professions.

Instead, they may want to enter into some other kind of interaction with the organization.

People can feel as though they belong, without having to be part of a club. Others may want that club affiliation. At the time the gift is made, find out how the donor wants to be recognized and involved. Make that information part of the database on that individual, and update it regularly through your ongoing relationship with the donor.

Be aware that some larger donors wish to be left alone except when *they* initiate contact with the organization. They will set the schedule: you need to be ready.

Combine cultivation and stewardship activities as much as possible -- the two functions are highly related. And, put donors and non-donors together as much as you can at special events.

A favorite cartoon shows a woman putting place cards around a large, beautifully appointed table. She is saying, "Donor, non-donor, donor, non-donor...." She is, of course, exactly right. Mix those who have given with those who are still thinking about it. The results will be beneficial to the individuals and to the organization.

If you're going to maintain truly long-term relationships that will benefit the organization over time, continue your stewardship practices even when an individual's giving flags.

As a rule, we base our stewardship strategies on internal measures of size or frequency of gifts. In most cases, this is appropriate. But board and staff should remember that a donor's circumstances may change temporarily. It is foolish to abandon the relationship with a funder who has given significantly in the past but has reduced or stopped giving.

If you have a good relationship with donors, you should know why they've changed their giving patterns. Chances are they'll be back — but not if you cut off your contact with them.

If you're no longer on their radar screen, you probably won't be funded when resources are available. Continued participation with your organization will influence future decisions about renewed sponsorships or contributions.

When creating stewardship programs, remember that people give to and become involved with your organization because of the program.

Create opportunities for donors to get to know the people who are using their investments to create programs and services in fulfillment of the mission of the organization. Involvement is deepened and commitment enhanced when donors become partners with those who actually provide the community service. Only then can they understand how their values are being acted on.

•••

Competition for resources in the nonprofit sector is going to increase as traditional sources of funding shrink. Donor loyalty is a known factor in successful organizations. Maintaining that loyalty is the principal goal of stewardship, and is its most powerful result.

17

EVALUATING YOUR FUNDRAISING EFFECTIVENESS

Sometimes, in the urgency of moving on to the next fundraising activity, analyzing the success of the previous one is overlooked. Did we raise the money? If so, what worked that we can do again? If not, what was the problem?

There are many ways to evaluate your fundraising effectiveness. Within the profession, benchmarks have been set. There are general formulas for calculating the cost of fundraising, and there are also organization-specific standards regarding the number and size of gifts you should bring in annually, and what constitutes a reasonable donor retention rate.

Taking these "hard" factors into consideration is of course very important. But there are other factors, too, some of which are "soft" and less measurable. These, too, need to be factored into the evaluation of any development program.

Without a balanced view of what constitutes effectiveness, it's difficult for development committees or boards to know if their fundraising efforts are working. And, it's difficult for development professionals to engage volunteers around an appropriate set of goals.

Here's what you should know about both the "hard" and "soft" sides of evaluating your fundraising effectiveness.

Set annual fundraising goals that are an "attainable-stretch."

Too often, fundraising goals are set by boards or administrators without the benefit of previous (and anticipated) performance indicators. They establish a goal that fills the gap between earned revenue and what's needed to run the organization, without regard to whether it's possible to raise the funds.

Setting a fundraising goal demands the involvement of development staff and volunteers in a careful analysis of previous fundraising campaigns, a survey of the current environment for fundraising, and a review of prospective current and lapsed donors.

It also requires knowledge of how many volunteers will be available for face-to-face asks, and what financial resources are needed for conducting direct mail campaigns, paying professionals to conduct telefunding, or staging large-scale fundraising events.

Fundraising effectiveness depends on factoring the right variables into your plan, and monitoring your progress regularly to adjust for changed circumstances. Stretch goals should be set systematically, not arbitrarily, and then actively pursued.

Acknowledge that fundraising events are best categorized as "friend raisers," and set your measures against two goals: to raise as much money and as many friends as possible.

Many organizations rely heavily on fundraising events. This often leads to disappointment, because event fundraising is subject to many perils, including timing, unexpected costs, lack of publicity, uneven volunteer leadership, and other factors that may slip out of control.

However, if fundraising events are seen for their other primary value -- as friend raisers -- then plans for measuring their effectiveness take on a new dimension.

Viewing events as friend raisers as well as fundraisers requires greater planning: attention during the event to those who are being cultivated as well as those who already have a relationship with the organization, post-event debriefs among volunteers and staff regarding what they saw and heard; and follow up with attendees through thank-you letters, phone calls and future involvement.

Measuring the effectiveness of fundraising events is more than just looking at net profit: it is also assessing how many new and continuing relationships were enhanced.

An important measure of fund raising effectiveness is how thoroughly the board and development committee own the goal and are involved in its achievement.

Fund raising cannot be considered effective when development professionals single-handedly — or with very few volunteers — raise all the money for an organization.

Truly effective programs are those that strategically involve board and other volunteers as well as administrative and program staff. These individuals should be involved in the planning, implementation, and evaluation phase of any fund raising drive, whether annual or capital.

Board members are the nucleus of any fund raising program. They inspire other volunteers to get involved, and buoy staff enthusiasm about being participants in the cultivation or the ask.

Board involvement leads to long-term stability for the program, and helps ensure that donors perceive a deep commitment within the organization to both the raising of funds and the appropriate management and distribution of those funds within the organization.

Fund raising effectiveness should also be measured by how many board members and other volunteers are willing to make face-to-face asks.

Board members and other community volunteers are the best people to contact others in the community about the organization. It isn't enough to write notes on letters or even to make a phone call. A mature fundraising program measures its effectiveness not only by money raised and calls made, but by how many people were willing to sit down with prospects and donors and ask for a gift.

Personal solicitations drive down the costs of fundraising by engaging volunteers in asking current donor-investors for large gifts and balancing the high cost of acquiring donors through direct mail or paid telephone solicitations.

The cost of fundraising is an aspect of development all fundraising professionals should watch carefully. If it's too high, donors will balk at giving. Keep it low by involving volunteers in the process.

A good fundraising program should raise your visibility in the community as well as increase donors.

Raising money is just the beginning. An annual program puts the mission out into the community and helps raise the visibility of that mission and the organization.

In one campaign involving two organizations that worked with women and children who had experienced domestic violence, a local advertising agency donated spot video and radio announcements as well as newspaper advertisements.

Their theme was, "Breaking the cycle of violence." It was a

blockbuster campaign and helped the two organizations significantly increase community awareness of their program. They also raised a considerable amount of money, which the two organizations shared equally.

The retention rate of donors is a critical measure.

If you have to start from scratch every year, trying to convince people to give, your fundraising program isn't very effective. The reason, usually, is because the focus is on raising money, not on developing relationships.

It's important to remember that donors are really investors: when they make a gift, the relationship begins (or renews). They're interested in the impact of their gift, the results the organization achieves, and they want to hear from you about the difference their gift made.

If you don't communicate with your donors until the next time you want money, it conveys the idea that you're only interested in getting money from them -- not in letting them know that you acknowledge their gift as a symbol of their belief in your purpose and your results.

Be sure your fundraising program is balanced, relying on funding from a variety of sources.

Most organizations have had to get away from government sources as primary funders, but find themselves overly relying on another single source like foundations or corporations. With the softening of the corporate sector, and the struggles of foundations with fluctuating portfolio value, these sources have also become less supportive. It's dangerous to rely on one primary source of funding at the exclusion of others. If that source bottoms out, the overall effectiveness is jeopardized. Be sure you are cultivating and soliciting from *all* constituencies.

In an effective program, people feel good about giving, and asking.

This is the softest, yet the hardest measure of success. If your volunteers and donors feel good, and you raise the money you set out to raise, then the program is effective at building the organization, community awareness, and the likelihood of continued investment in the organization is great.

If your volunteers are irreparably burned out at the end of an annual or capital campaign, it hasn't been effective no matter how much money you've raised.

Renewal of volunteers is essential. Along the way, they're bound to get tired, frustrated or discouraged. However, staff and board leadership support for volunteers should be such that these feelings are fleeting.

Recognize your volunteers in the way that's appropriate for their accomplishment and personal needs; mete out their assignments so they aren't overwhelmed; help them when they seem discouraged; encourage them when they're doubtful or worried; provide professional advice and counsel to help them improve their skills; give them training and coaching to improve their effectiveness; and let them know how important they are by measuring the impact of their service in terms of the accomplishments of your organization.

Remember that there are two bottom lines in philanthropy: the financial return and the values return.

In an effective program, both bottom lines are honored and strong. In reporting your results and measuring your effectiveness, measure not only the money, but measure the impact on the mission as well. The mission embodies the needs of the community and inspires the investment.

An effective fundraising program is based on a belief in the importance of the mission to the community, the urgency of the need that's being met (not the urgent need for funds), and views all gifts as investments and all donors as values-driven investors.

Honor the gifts and the values they represent, and, when reporting your successes to your donors, remember to tell the stories that convey the impact of their generosity. It will be the highest measure of your effectiveness.

•••

There are many measures of effectiveness in fundraising. Take them all into consideration when setting your goals, monitoring your programs, and conducting your campaign evaluation or year-end reporting.

18

FUNDRAISING IN A CHANGING ECONOMY

The economic balloon may not have burst, but certainly it's leaking. Newspapers carry daily stories about massive layoffs, plummeting earnings, and gloomy predictions for future recovery. The stock market zooms up and down like a roller coaster, and a few economic indices have plunged and rested at the bottom without significant recovery.

During the robust days of the dot.com economic boom, we spoke often and optimistically about a golden age of philanthropy. We imagined continuing great partnerships with wealthy visionaries of all ages who would see the power of investing in their communities. And yet, today, the scene seems to have changed.

Corporate philanthropy programs have reduced staffing and grants, large and small foundations report slimmer earnings and less money to give, and many individuals – whether directly affected by the economic slump or not – are unsure about the future and more conservative with their nonprofit investments.

How can you work most effectively in this current shifting economy – fulfilling mission, sustaining investors, and making adjustments that may become necessary if the current patterns continue?

Put another way:

• How can you maintain relationships with significant donors who may be unable to continue their generous support?

• How can you creatively structure opportunities for philanthropic involvement for people whose confidence in their own economic power may be eroded? And,

• What is the best way to retain a relationship with a funder that will put your name at the top of the funding list when times get better?

Here are the most important things to know about doing business as a nonprofit in a volatile economy.

Remember that philanthropy is more than giving money.

In uncertain economic times, position your organization so that opportunities for asking, joining, and serving are as evident as opportunities to give.

Engage current and lapsed donors in ways that keep them connected to your mission and give you leverage in the community. If someone has made a significant gift, and now finds resources more scarce, coach them in how to become an advocate-asker: drawing on their own reasons for supporting your organization in persuasive meetings with those who can give new or renewed support.

If someone who used to be a funder is out of work and feeling embarrassed or uncomfortable – show them that your interest in them is much deeper than as a donor. Involve them in a volunteer job (strategic planning, marketing) that calls on their professional expertise, gives you the benefit of their wisdom, and keeps their skills sharp until the next great job comes along.

Be more accountable and transparent than ever.

People whose resources are limited -- as well as people with greater assets -- want to make their investments where they know they will have the biggest impact.

We know that we need to be accountable, that our results must be measurable, that one of the key aspects of current philanthropy is the need to be transparent. This is even more imperative in a soft economy.

Nonprofits can and must convey to prospects and donors what the impact of their gift will be, how that impact will be measured, and how that measurement will be conveyed.

Future Shock, written at another time of economic transition, referred to that era as an uncertain time, but "a great and yeasty time" in which new things were possible.

As nonprofits, we need to welcome, not resist, the demand for evaluation and accountability. But we need to know our own marketplace and programs so well that we can convey what the appropriate measures are. We need to define the benchmarks and peg our progress to them.

Convey a sincere commitment to long-time donors based on the belief that an investment has a long life.

Too often, we drop people from our stewardship and recognition programs when their gift lapses. What this conveys is a short-cycle view of investment. If someone makes a significant gift that allows you to develop a program, expand your season, hire new people – then the residual of that gift continues to have an impact long after the gift itself is spent.

The notion of gifts as investments requires us to take a longer view of return on that investment. When a funder isn't able to make the level of gift (or any gift) for one or more years, don't drop them from your lists or your events. Economic cycles are inevitable, and you want to be at the top of that funder's list when times get better.

Your organization may also find itself having to cut staff.

If you find yourself in that position, do it wisely, legally, and with heart. Eliminate the position, not the person. Let people know how difficult this is. Convey to the community what the cuts will mean. Be transparent with your funders and clients about the difficulty of the decision and the ways in which you will "backfill" to ensure the best possible service delivery.

And, as a side benefit to an otherwise painful process, crank up your volunteer program wherever possible and appropriate. Many organizations, able to staff up with additional resources in more abundant times, have found themselves using fewer volunteers or using them in different ways.

The slogan, "when life gives you lemons, make lemonade" has application here. Make the volunteer experience one that is rewarding – and where you can match the out-of-work person with the "out-of-person" work that needs to be done in your organization, you have a winning combination!

If you haven't been good stewards of small gifts and their givers, get busy!

The Golden Age of philanthropy was ushered in and characterized by gifts that were very large from people who may never have made a gift to a particular organization. Because philanthropy is increasingly issues-driven, these were people who sought to make a difference in an area of philanthropic importance to them. They chose an organization and offered it an opportunity to do something significant with a major infusion of funds.

In the process, organizations have had to be careful not to focus just on these big gifts, but to honor and value smaller gifts and their givers as well. But, let's face it. If you have limited funding for stewardship (mailings, events, personal outreach) you will spend it on the people who have given the most.

Nevertheless, there is still a great deal to be said for people who start with modest gifts and move up the giving pyramid with incrementally larger gifts.

Take care of them now more than ever before. When the next high cycle occurs, they could be your big donors. And, be sure to include those major (even lapsed) donors in the same stewardship program. Keep them close, and keep them involved.

Look for hidden or impervious-to-change wealth in your community.

Seasoned development professionals know that sometimes the greatest wealth isn't obvious. The last several years of incredible economic growth have created many new sources of wealth and many new wealthy individuals. The majority of them are still intact, and many of them are still to be identified.

Watch the transfer of wealth in your community and engage these new potential donors – particularly women and people of color – in dialogue about what your organization is doing to meet the needs of the community. Uncover their values and connect them with what you're doing. Be a watcher and a reader and a listener.

Keep cultivating – the cycle will recycle.

Beyond the hidden or impervious wealth, and the temporarily lapsed or reduced donors, lies another whole untapped world of potential support. You'll discover it by looking upon this time as a time of donor acquisition. But don't resort to direct mail exclusively: think instead of how you market your organization, the messages you send, the materials you use, the events you sponsor, the ways in which you involve yourself directly in the community.

All of this is cultivation – and can be followed by more systematic and deliberate cultivation of those who step forward and identify themselves as interested in what you are doing. They are your next generation of funders and volunteers.

Be prudent in your own organization's financial planning.

Many of your board members are well aware of having to scrutinize and pinch back the budgets in their own homes and organizations. Make sure your organizational budget reflects that same kind of process. None of us can know when the balloon is going to re-inflate – or whether it will deflate completely. But, prudent planning that reflects knowledge of the fragile market-place will impress your board members and funders. Don't stay fat when your funders are growing lean.

Look to new markets, including your earned income stream.

Evaluate your sources of earned income (client fees, subscriptions, single tickets, bookstore, or thrift shop) and see if you can cut your margins there to increase your yield.

Increasingly, nonprofits need to look beyond pure philanthropic dollars to ways they can leverage potential sources of earned income to balance the need for philanthropic dollars.

If you have an endowment, or even a reserve fund, make sure it's invested safely but wisely. That, too, can increase your income and convey a message that you're aware of market volatility and the need to balance income sources. All of which positions you as a better investment for those who can invest.

Consider different timing for your mailings and major donor campaigns.

If everyone in your community solicits in November, why don't you solicit in September? If most events are held in the spring, why not do yours in the winter? Get "off cycle" so that people don't have to make tough decisions for their discretionary dollars. Keep track of the major events in the community, and plan yours around them.

Watch when the greatest influx of direct mail occurs, and plan yours for a different time. We usually think of summer as a bad time to fundraise, but one organization in a resort community always used that time for their local business campaign. The businesses were riding high, and so did their campaign.

●●●

The Golden Age of philanthropy isn't over; it has just begun. What happened in the past few years isn't going to go away. If money is more scarce, or if people are more cautious, we need to show that we have both patience and opportunities through these times. We have much to work with even if the dollars are reduced.

Donors are better educated about philanthropy, organizations are better positioned, communities are more aware of our impact and the needs we meet, and society is more open to the ways in which effective donor investment in nonprofits can change people, institutions, and communities. We need to show that we're a robust part of a still vigorous economy, and provide continuing opportunities for investment that go beyond money.

19

OVERCOMING YOUR DONORS' PSYCHIC POVERTY

The roller coaster ride of the American stock market lost its entertainment value a while ago! Long-awaited recovery is slow to take hold.

Although there's a certain philosophical acceptance of the market's cyclical nature, and guarded optimism that the bottom isn't going to last, the news about market performance -- and even the value of the dollar against foreign currencies -- has been the same grim news.

An interesting and challenging outgrowth of the recent hammering of investments is the psychological impact it has on those who invest not only in companies, but also in nonprofit organizations.

These people – whether their income and net worth are large or small experience "psychic poverty" – a feeling of scarcity, rather than abundance. And while those who became fabulously wealthy (relative to their previous status) in the 90s are still much wealthier than before, the gap between their current and previous wealth is alarming to many.

Even people who aren't invested in the stock market – whose

holdings are in real estate or in their own companies – or who have no holdings at all – feel the pressure of uncertainty.

This spills over into their philanthropic commitments, and they become hesitant about committing large sums or renewing previous support "until the economy gets better." That may take a while, and there are community needs to be met. So what is the best strategy?

Here's what you should know about helping people through a tough time of feeling psychic poverty. If you are successful, you will help them, and help your organization as well.

Recognize that people are honestly worried about the future.

While we see hopeful signs here and there in the economy, the truth is, this has been a very challenging time. Don't try to talk people out of what they're observing and experiencing – you'll sound like a slick salesman, not a professional or a peer.

In times like these, it is good to remember that we all have two ears and one mouth, and to use them in that ratio. Most people just want to be heard: they have views on everything from economics to terrorism to local issues in your community. Give them a way and place to be heard.

Grace (Episcopal) Cathedral in San Francisco has been particularly successful at this, both through its on-site gatherings and through Grace.com. The forum they provide has retained for their constituency the intellectual, spiritual, social, and emotional involvement that is clearly needed by many at this time.

Be genuinely accepting of comments, even among the still very wealthy, that they feel poor.

There's a relative aspect to feeling poor: some feel it, some don't. Someone worth millions, now worth only half of that amount, may feel poor.

In our family, during the Great Depression, one of my father's aunts was married to a clergyman who died at 37 leaving her with five children and no money. They were very poor. One day her children came home and told their mother there was a food drive for the "poor" at school. They wanted to bring something.

Aunt Maggie went to her cupboard and found some cans of soup – ones she could hardly afford to give away – and sent them to school. Her children never knew they were poor, because they had never had much to begin with and because Aunt Maggie always focused on the things they *had*, rather than what they did *not* have.

Recently, with the decline in relative (and absolute wealth), people are painfully aware of what they no longer have. We need to accommodate this, while beginning to position our mission and issues as worthy of even diminished investment.

Emphasize the relative safety of an investment in your organization.

As people mourn their risky investments in now-dead or dying companies and industries, we can mount a good communications program based on the impact of investments in our organizations. Returning to what we know works – focusing on results, not needs – we can show that our ROI (return on investment) is fantastic.

Lives are altered, communities are bettered, children are fed and clothed, people are housed, and great art and music fill our halls – all as a result of community investment.

Glide Memorial Methodist Church in San Francisco – a major spiritual and social center – put up a few well-placed billboards in San Francisco in 2002, offering their programs as a safe place to invest. This was particularly appropriate for this center of the dot.com boom, but in other communities across America a similar message about our nonprofits' return on investment needs to be stressed.

As well as emphasizing the safety of an investment in your organization, communicate the *impact* an investment has.

This can be a time for instituting some notable shifts in the way people think about their money and its uses. It could be that one of the permanent benefits of a time of extreme readjustment is the realization that a "balanced portfolio" is a metaphor for life.

As we read stories of those who survived the World Trade Tower tragedy or other life-threatening events or diseases, we realize that the ultimate answer for many of them has been to simplify and savor. Philanthropic investment provides that opportunity, too.

Get a fresh start on the way you communicate with your investors. Even if you've already mastered the importance of conveying impact, not needs, use more human interest stories. Keep them simple and to the point.

Illustrate your rehab program's impact by having a person whose life was changed write your annual appeal letter. Bring people who have benefited from your programs to donor receptions and to special events. Have them speak briefly at key gatherings.

Years ago, a children's service agency had a very high profile speaker come to its 40th anniversary celebration and talk about major trends in child development. Impressive, but not nearly so much as the young man in his 30s who spoke from his heart about his years in their care from the age of 2 to 10, and how it had changed his life. Now self-supporting with a family, he said he owed it all to them.

There were few dry eyes in the room.

There has never been a better time to practice good donor and community outreach.

Not only are people seeking a sense of community as we consider what's happened to us globally and as a country, they're also looking for stable values-based organizations that will serve as ballast during these stormy times.

Assure them that yours is just such an organization.

Spend more time reaching out and letting people know that as a result of their investment in your organization lives have been enriched. Use the Internet and other venues to share your success stories. We're all searching for the good in the news these days. Be proactive in providing it.

If you're in an area where there's high unemployment, think of ways to involve those whose work is gone or has changed.

One organization benefited itself and several key supporters who had lost their jobs in the "dot.bomb" experience in California.

These individuals, without work but with some short-term financial stability, turned their energy towards volunteering. They were ably guided by the organization and given new responsibilities that enhanced their sense of self-worth.

Concerned about their financial future, they no longer continued their generous gifts – but the time and talent they provided were a significant investment.

As the tide turns, they will be back among the financial contributors as well – having set their psychic poverty aside with a new job or career.

As you work with donors individually to help them feel included, cared for, and engaged with the ongoing work in which

they've invested, gauge the time when you can ask them to become your ally and champion.

Ours is a sector that relies heavily on peer interaction. It's the basis of our governance and our development programs. Make it the basis, as well, for inviting those who have either passed through their own feeling of psychic poverty – or who never felt it but are sympathetic to those who do – to become allies with you in developing strategies for helping others.

Get their permission to publicize gifts they've made during this time. Ask them to speak informally at board meetings. Have them accompany you on calls to family foundations and to individuals where they can provide their own "from the heart" account of how and why they contributed.

Encourage them to become informal advocates and have them talk about creative ways to sustain support even when cash flow trickles: by volunteering, asking others to give, getting people to join, and attending events.

Because fundraising is about relationships rather than money, this is an opportune time to show that we practice what we believe.

This may be our test time. The too-frequent complaint among donors is that we only contact them when we want money. Well, now is our chance to disprove this.

Keep those who have suspended their support in the loop regarding their previous investments. If we truly believe in the investment theory of giving, then what they previously invested in (a life, a program, a project, a discovery, a concert) still has residual benefit in the community and the organization.

The fact that they choose not to give now, while their stock portfolio, company, small business or other income is suffering, is no reason to abandon these supporters. We need to honor them and keep them involved.

If some people continue to cite lack of wealth as their reason for not giving, even when recovery seems imminent, look to other reasons for their disconnection.

Sometimes people find excuses not to continue their philanthropy, often because they feel disconnected from the values, vision, or mission of the organization. If this is the case, and if you've honestly tried to keep them engaged through difficult times, it's probably a signal to let them go.

Remember, however, that these people will always be investors in your organization, even if they're not currently involved.

From time to time, let them know what you're doing, what your successes are, and that their previous investment was important. Who knows, they just might come back.

Be a model for the larger economic sector through your integrity, transparency, and values.

The excesses and abuses of power and the denial of investor rights this past year have been rampant.

As a vital, vigorous, and important part of the economic balance in our society, let people know that the public benefit (nonprofit) sector is committed to investor return, community involvement, and management approaches that are measured by the impact on the community.

Although we must attain and preserve a strong financial bottom line, it is not our only measure. We also must deliver on our investor's and community values.

By living our values, we'll not only raise donor confidence and increase investor satisfaction, we'll also position our sector as a healthy, robust, and delightful place to invest.

•••

As the economic cycle wavers, falls and rises, only to fall again, attention to your donors has never been more important. Their feeling of psychic poverty needn't be fatal, however, if you employ the strategies detailed here to keep them involved through challenging times.

20

HIRING DEVELOPMENT STAFF

Making the right hiring decision has always been tough. But, to make it even more difficult, we've seen a recent shift from a buyer's market to a seller's market in nonprofit development positions.

Even a casual reader of any current national, regional, or local publication that lists development-related job openings is aware of the shortage of qualified people across the country and across disciplines.

Increasingly, professionals in search of staff find themselves looking to new sources outside the sector, often with a great deal of worry about how people without development experience will fare in the nonprofit pressure cooker.

Others network intensively with fellow professionals, but are fearful of the risk in raiding another organization's staff.

Still others put off hiring, waiting for the market to break, and use consultants or volunteers to keep the annual or capital funding programs afloat.

The reasons for the shortage, and for our inability to bridge the gap between open positions and people to fill them, are complex. Some have to do with the way our sector is viewed, some with the way our organizations are perceived to be structured and managed, some have to do with lower than market salaries, and some originate from the way we manage the hiring process – beginning with the job description and continuing through the job offer and the orientation.

Here's what you should know about hiring development staff, especially if it's a tough market in your community.

Be sure the job description is current and clear.

This probably seems so elementary you're wondering why it's included here. The truth is, most job descriptions are poorly thought out.

If the job is one that has been previously held, the tendency is to "find Ruth's replacement." No attempt is made to figure out if Ruth was doing the right job for the organization at that time.

Resist this tendency and instead give yourself the luxury of some zero-based thinking: what jobs do we need to do, who are our existing people, what are their talents, how would they like to be assigned, what would motivate them and, given that we need an additional staff person, what should that job be?

This is an energizing process for staff members: they will be more motivated and feel, in many ways, that their job is "new," too.

By the same token, if the job is a new position, develop the job description by consulting with existing staff about what they would like this new person to do and to be like.

Transitions in staffing, while time consuming and sometimes difficult, can be opportunities for redefining *all* jobs, not just the one being filled. Even though other job descriptions may not change substantially, people will feel as though their job has been reaffirmed.

And, if they have found some new work to do that is motivating, you'll have a more productive staff overall.

This exercise may even lead to the happy conclusion that you can promote from within, thereby giving others incentives to stick around.

While you're drafting the job description and ad for this position, do a little internal marketing with the board and administration to raise the respect and the salaries for the development function.

We spend most of our time marketing to our community, and too little time letting people within our organizations know the impact of the development function. I'm not suggesting you become a shameless self-promoter, ultimately doing more harm than good.

Instead, you should be continuously communicating within your organization the grants you bring in, the major gifts you've cultivated, the increase in membership, the visits from dignitaries and funders, favorable press that busy program people might have missed.

Position this new or just-vacant job in the context of everything you're accomplishing, and let people know how important it is.

Make the expectations realistic: explain that relationship building is the precursor to fundraising, and that a new person (if she is a "front line" fundraiser) will have to get to know people before an impact is felt on the bottom line.

If the new person is support staff, patience is also required: he or she will not know the names of all the important parties immediately.

Finally, take a look at all salary and benefit packages in the development office, compare them to similar organizations in your community if possible, and persuade the budget-makers that this position, in order to attract the calibre of person needed, should have a higher salary.

It may not work if there are demands on the budget beyond your control, but it's a healthy exercise relative to the overall respect for the development process.

Look for potential candidates outside the traditional sources and experience pools.

Development is a challenging job: we all know that. And, because we tend to focus on knowledge and experience rather than the *qualities* of a person, we get frustrated when we don't find that ideal fit with the list of qualifications we're looking for.

Think outside these qualifications. Think of the kind of person you want: flexible, creative, mature, decision-maker, self-starter, great communicator, ability to both lead and follow, capable of working across several departments and with volunteers. And, if she also knows how to run an annual fund, that's a bonus.

In my years of hiring I've found that even if she lacks experience, I would rather have someone who is smart, flexible, and motivated as opposed to a technician who knows how to conduct a direct mail campaign but lacks the qualities to make her a success in our organization.

Think about the backgrounds and experience that can transfer to our sector: marketing, advertising, teaching, other professions that require communication and the ability to work with a wide variety of people and situations.

Be open to looking beyond our sector for experience. Network with marketing organizations and other related professional people. You may find an ideal candidate who has little or no development experience but in whom you see great potential and are willing to invest in training. And, there are some very talented people looking for meaningful work. Check them out.

Look for qualities, not just qualifications.

People fail in jobs not because they attended the wrong university or didn't have the requisite three to five years experience at a similar institution. They fail because they don't have the intellectual or interpersonal attributes, or a sufficient energy level, to get the job done.

Harvard professor Harry Levinson provided the employment world with the behavioral job description decades ago. In this approach to defining a position, Levinson admonished managers making hiring decisions to define not only the knowledge and experience required, but also the intellectual and interpersonal skills and the energy they're looking for.

It is around these qualities, Levinson asserts, that most failures occur.

Take time to define the qualities as well as the qualifications, and circulate these among the people who will be interviewing your candidates.

Get some training in interviewing.

Most managers are miserable interviewers. We give away the store by telling candidates too much about the organization at the outset of the interview – and then are thrilled by how well they match what the organization is looking for.

We telegraph answers ("Here at Children's Services International, we look for people with high integrity and great flexibility in their work style. Are those attributes you would bring to our organization?") What do you think they're going to say to that?

We talk too much, and don't listen. Remember you have two

ears and one mouth: use them in that ratio while interviewing (just like you do when soliciting a gift!).

Often, we attain our interviewing skills as managers by remembering those who interviewed us. Guess what? Most of them had no training, and were making it up as they went along. We can do better. Get some training. Read a professional book.

Remember that candidates will have spent half the day preparing for the interview – while you, as a busy manager, may have forgotten that you had an interview scheduled, have trouble finding the resume on your desk, and be totally unprepared. The advantage, in such an interview, will not be yours.

Make sure the hiring process has integrity and shows respect for the candidates.

Too many organizations display arrogance in the hiring process, albeit inadvertent. By failing to communicate with candidates about the process, keeping them waiting, putting them through poorly structured interviews, not letting them know whether they're still a candidate, and by not thanking them graciously for their time even though there's no position for them, we convey arrogance and an impression of our organization (and our sector) that is irreversible.

We cannot afford to alienate anyone who comes to us with interest. Remember that the hiring process is a marketing process for you and for the nonprofit sector.

Involve the right people in the interview process, but don't go overboard.

It's important that people who will interact with them interview final candidates. The board chair, development chair, CEO, CFO, and selected others need to be participants. However, don't make the process so complex that it appears you're disseminating the risk of the hiring decision.

Some companies and nonprofits have literally dozens of people, individually and in panels, who meet with final candidates. The process takes days, and then the decision takes weeks because everyone has to be consulted.

Ultimately, this dilutes the decision-making process and can convey to the candidate that yours is an organization that has difficulty making decisions and taking responsibility for them. Keep the process swift but thorough, and keep it on a timetable that you convey to the candidate.

Be honest and open with final candidates.

If you have a great candidate you want to hire, by all means sell her on the sector and the organization. Tell her about the passion and the satisfactions, let her know there are non-monetary compensations for working in the sector that, at the end of the day, are more valuable than money.

But, while doing this, don't paint a picture that slights the truth. In our attempt to sell a promising candidate, we tend to gloss over the very things that will eventually be points of concern or departure: the real expectations.

This has to do with everything from describing the real issues around the workload, to working with the board, to accurately and objectively depicting everything from the financial statements, to the idiosyncrasies of your board or staff.

Transparency is in. Let your new employee become a partner in implementing your mission by presenting portions of the job as a pleasure filled with opportunity but revealing the parts of the job that will be a challenge. No surprises.

Once the person is hired, give him a decent orientation and

start-up period.

When I transitioned from a development director's job in social services to a development position in higher education, it was a big shift. But when I arrived at the new job for the first day of work I had flowers, but no boss. He was away for a week. No one really knew I was coming (he had sent the flowers by wire), and the first week was very frustrating.

I found my way around, but missed that welcoming immersion that sets the tone for the way people interact. There was, I soon realized, a solitary mindset on the part of the staff: each person doing his or her own job, and not much linkage from job to job. It was a culture that ultimately proved unsatisfying.

When a person is welcomed, introduced, oriented to the facility and to the administrative and program staff – and assured that there's a support system within the organization – then higher productivity and confidence results.

Be diligent about the separation of board and staff responsibilities.

One sure way to cause a talented person who's new to our sector – or someone who's a veteran from another organization — to leave an organization is for the board to micro-manage individuals or departments.

Hiring a new person is a good time to have a quick session with the board about the line of demarcation between board and staff in development. By tying it into the new position, it seems less of a lecture and more of an orientation for the board.

At the same time, be sure that board members don't perceive increased staff as decreased responsibilities for them. In fact, it may mean increased responsibilities. If you, at last, are able to bring on a director of stewardship, then board members will be much more actively involved in the stewardship process.

•••

Beyond the hiring process, there is the continued diligence of performance evaluation, regular fine-tuning of the position to maintain motivation, and a commitment to ongoing professional development so that the person stays energized about the impact of our sector.

Hiring and keeping good people is increasingly challenging, but these suggestions can help you get a good start with a new employee.

21

HIRING A DEVELOPMENT OR ORGANIZATIONAL CONSULTANT

At some time or another, nearly every nonprofit needs to hire a development or organizational consultant. It may be for a capital campaign, for strategic planning, for organizational issues with board or staff, to facilitate a board retreat, or to conduct an assessment of development systems and practices.

Making the decision to bring in a consultant is relatively easy. A situation or opportunity arises within the organization that, by its nature or needs, requires outside assessment, counsel, or facilitation. Staff, or the board, or both agree to hire someone experienced at working with similar situations in other organizations. And they set out on their search for a consultant.

But while the decision to hire may be easy, the search can be quite confusing - especially if it is the first time you've sought counsel, or sought counsel for this particular purpose. Just sorting through the array of consultants is itself a challenge.

As you would expect, consultants come in all sizes, shapes, and dispositions. Some call themselves organizational consultants, some say they're development consultants, others are planning consultants, and still others are fundraising or campaign consultants.

They may be from a "one-person shop" or part of a larger firm with local, state, or national offices. They charge by the job, the day, the month, or the hour. Some incorporate expenses, others itemize them, still others build them in as a percentage of the contract.

The duration of a consultant's service will also vary widely. Some consultations are as short as a half-day (board or staff training session) and others go on for years (board development, staff development, capital campaigns). Some have ironclad contracts that reflect legal training or advice; others operate on a verbal contract or handshake.

With this variation in consulting types, arrangements, length of service, and the way in which they are deployed in organizations, it is important to know the basic factors to consider when hiring such a person. Here, then, are important things to know about hiring a development or organizational consultant.

Take time to focus on the desired outcomes, as well as the desired process, when formulating the recruitment strategy for hiring the consultant.

Before approaching any consultant, be sure your outcomes are clearly identified. Then you will know - from the confusing array of consultant labels - whether you need development, fundraising, organizational, strategic planning, or other kinds of consultation.

Identifying your desired outcome - whether it's a board retreat, help with strategic planning, or a capital campaign - also helps you create better measures for the interview process and for the eventual evaluation of the consultation.

If, to use the example of a board retreat, your objective is to identify basic goals for a strategic plan, to create closer communication among board members, and to build board and staff understanding of mutual responsibilities, then you can ask the consultant directly how he or she would facilitate each of those outcomes. The interview will be more revealing, and the decision easier, if these specifics are discussed.

Use your network and your community resources to identify and screen possible consultants.

It's relatively easy to find information about consultants others have used for similar purposes. If you're part of a formal network (AFP, CASE, NAIS, AHP), there are usually local or national consultant directories available (some are on the Internet).

In many locations, community and private foundations maintain a consultant directory with listings according to types of consulting and typical clients and fees.

In a growing number of communities, there are nonprofit management centers that also maintain lists of consultants. Some even provide consultants directly, often for a lesser fee than an independent consultant charges.

Informal networking is also effective, of course, and colleagues in other organizations will usually give you candid information about consultants with whom they've worked.

Even if the consultation is to be brief (a board retreat, for example) or highly focused (staff training in time management), be sure to do a thorough interviewing job.

Mistakes in hiring a consultant hurt the organization in two ways: the time and money are wasted and, later on, when a consultant may be needed again, no one wants to hire one.

The process is simple. When you have completed the research to see who in your community (or outside your community) provides the kind of consultation you need, develop a list of names of individuals who seem, by experience or reputation, to fit what you're looking for. Have a mix of big firms and independent consultants, so you can compare resources and approach when you interview and make your decision. Call colleagues and ask if they know any of the candidates.

Conduct telephone interviews (they provide an initial insight into the candidate's communication skills). If you like the telephone interview, ask for a written proposal (these offer insights into organizational skills, respect for deadlines, verbal skills), and then follow up with a face-to-face interview.

If the consultation will involve the board, be sure the key players on the board are involved in the interview. If the consultation is for a capital campaign consultant, include key development, administrative, and board representatives in the interview. And, remember, focus the questions around your desired outcomes from the consultation.

When planning to work with a consultant, for any purpose, be sure the entire staff understands the purpose of the consultation, the desired outcomes, the estimated duration of the consultation, and what their involvement will be (if any).

Sadly, consultants can be viewed as a threat. If their purpose is not explained, and if there's no knowledge of or buy-in for the goals of the consultation, it can lead to non-cooperation based in fear or resentment.

Discuss the proposed consultation with staff. If it is for strategic planning, tell them what the process will be (interviews, meetings, a retreat) and the approximate duration of the process. Let them know how much time you will expect from them.

If it is for a capital campaign, be very clear at the outset how demanding a campaign is and why a consultant can help achieve the goals and relieve the chaos. Some consultants, because of their experience or reputation - or because of the length of their contract with you - will require large budget allocations. Therefore, the importance of the outcomes of the consultation to the overall capacity of the organization needs to be stressed.

Too often, communication about a consultation is only with the development office or administration. Program staff also need to be informed: after all, the whole purpose of making an organization run more effectively or raise significant dollars is to grow the program!

Rely on research, experience, references, insights, rapport and chemistry in making your decision about which consultant to hire.

These decisions are highly specific to each organization. The person who was just right for one organization may be completely wrong for another. Know your organization, and know what it needs.

Sometimes, it's hard to know what is best. An organization with fragile or inadequate infrastructure that is approaching a capital campaign will have to "assemble the bicycle while riding it."

If, however, the board of that organization is comprised of people impatient with process who just want to get out and ask for money, the kind of consultant you would choose in the first example would be inappropriate. In that case, a phased consultation using two distinctly different individuals may be in order: one to work systemically within the organization; the other to get out into the community with board members and raise the money. One process (and consultant) is transformational; the other is transactional.

Know what you need before choosing your consultant.

While discussing the big picture, and the outcomes, be sure not to pass over the details (like fees).

Some consultants are very compelling and charismatic in their presentations, and it's easy to get swept up in their vision. This quality is excellent, particularly for facilitation or training sessions with board or staff.

However, somewhere in the interview, ask them to review the details of their proposal: fees, contracts, schedules, staff resources in their offices, and timelines, including other consulting work that may delay yours.

Knowing this information before you hire the consultant can help you make a more informed decision. Don't get your heart set on a consultant you can't afford (although, increasingly, community foundations and other funders are interested in capacity building and will fund the cost of a consultant and the follow-up work for board training, strategic planning, staff development, and other systemic issues).

Look for different qualities according to the type of consultation.

If this is a long-term capital project, starting with a feasibility study, where the consultant will have a great deal of interaction with your board, staff, and the community, be sure the person wears well.

Talk to others who have used the consultant. Conduct more than one interview. Be sure the chemistry checks out with the key players on your team. Also, if you've chosen a larger firm, and another consultant is going to work with the lead consultant, it's important to meet that person as well.

Related to this issue is the importance of determining who spends what amount of time with you. There have been unfortunate situations where the lead consultant didn't show up at all after a while, leaving the project in the hands of a second consultant who didn't have the chemistry or experience to give the client confidence.

Draft a Letter of Agreement or contract, no matter how short the consultation is.

It is tempting, with a board or staff retreat or training, just to make a verbal agreement, or to trade e-mails, or to agree at the end of a face-to-face meeting. But it's important to have a letter of agreement or contract for every outside service you engage.

In this letter or contract you include the desired outcomes of the consultation, the client and consultant expectations, timeline, conditions for termination of the agreement by either party, fees and expenses, amount of time to be spent by the lead consultant, and other pertinent information including a description of the "deliverables."

It doesn't have to be complicated, or advised by a lawyer. Both parties sign the letter or contract, and each keeps a copy. Use the completed letter of agreement as a way to keep the consultation on schedule. It signals the importance and professionalism of the consultation, and provides excellent record keeping for the organization and the consultant.

If the consultation is long-term, build benchmarks into the agreement to measure progress.

Long-term arrangements of any kind tend to drift if they aren't evaluated periodically. If, going into the agreement, the client and consultant know they're going to be working together for a period of several years, incorporate benchmarks and review periods into the letter of agreement or contract.

At these sessions, review the progress towards outcomes. Make adjustments as needed. Let the consultant and the client speak candidly about what's working and what isn't.

Benchmarking can be done in one-on-one meetings, or can be built into quarterly or semi-annual sessions with the board.

Some contracts can be written so that the consultation is in phases, with evaluation criteria established for the completion of each phase.

And after you've hired the consultant, if you expect him to keep up his side of the bargain, be sure you keep up yours.

If you expect the consultant to keep up his or her side of the bargain, be sure you keep up yours. There are numerous ways that client actions or delays can derail or destroy a consulting arrangement.

If a consultant needs information about the organization to prepare for a meeting, delays in receiving it can throw a timeline into disarray. Clients that agree to release invitation letters for a feasibility study at a certain time — a time pegged to dates the consultant has kept open to conduct interviews — may delay the study by months if they do not get the letters out on schedule.

Failure to inform the consultant of changes at the organization or of events that have bearing on the consultation can put the consultant in a difficult position with key individuals whose confidence is critical.

Maintain agreements, keep promises, and make sure the consultant has both the environment and the tools to be effective.

•••

Engaging a consultant, at the right time for your organization, can be enormously productive and effective. These suggestions should help you make a better decision and help you manage the process more ably.

Part Two

◆

BOARD AND ORGANIZATIONAL DEVELOPMENT

22

RECRUITING AND ENLISTING THE BEST BOARD POSSIBLE

Every nonprofit organization dreams of recruiting, enlisting, and maintaining a board of trustees that will be wise decision-makers, visionary planners, able advocates, generous investors, willing askers, informed partners, and passionate pragmatists. Putting together such a board is not an impossible dream.

Dynamic board development is the proven key to successful organizational growth and fund development (which is why the board development committee is the most important committee of the board).

Too many boards are assembled without a strategy. Board selection is pushed by a date by which "a slate" must be presented. Frenzied phone calls result in the inappropriate recruitment of people who may be well-intentioned, but may not be the ones who can propel the organization to the next level.

Those recruited in haste are often assured that there's "nothing to it" (being on the board). They are told such things as, "You don't have to do anything but come to meetings," or "We just need your name," or (the worst), "We're desperate to submit a full slate of board nominees – please say yes."

Here's what you should know about identifying, recruiting, enlisting and retaining a top quality board.

Rebalance the recruitment equation.

Traditional recruitment practices have the same flaw as traditional fundraising practices: they position the organization's needs ahead of the needs of the community or prospective board member.

Just as we fundraise out of desperation until we understand that it's an investment process based in values and filled with opportunity, we frequently recruit out of desperation until we understand that board development is also an investment process. Rebalancing the equation requires us to change our strategy.

Recruit from a sense of pride in your organization. Don't assume that people *won't* want to serve; make them feel as though it's a great opportunity for them to serve their community and work with people who share their values.

Don't minimize the seriousness of being a board member: approach candidates as though it is a serious undertaking from which you feel they, and your organization, will benefit greatly.

Don't minimize the commitment required. Set standards for board performance. Let people know that this is an organization that values its volunteers and expects them to give their time, their expertise, and their financial support.

In short, develop a new and positive attitude about the recruitment process.

Develop a board recruitment matrix, based on your institutional plan.

In your institutional plan, you have focused areas in development, marketing, program, stewardship, and outreach. To fulfill the goals and objectives of your plan, you will need board members with special skills and connections to work with staff (or, if you have very few paid staff, to supplement staff work) in developing strategy and creating community linkages.

Profile your existing board, assessing such areas as profession, expertise, willingness to ask, connections in the community, knowledge of your mission and purpose.

You may also want to profile your board by age, race, geography, gender, and other indicators that are often important to funders when assessing how well your board reflects your community or constituency.

With the profile, or matrix, of the existing board complete, compare it to the needs revealed in your institutional plan.

If you need more people who are good community fundraisers, recruit among the ranks of people who have experience with other organizations. If you need more corporate connections, you may need to add a few corporate board members. If marketing is a high priority, add that to the matrix. If your board lacks diversity of gender, age, geography or race, indicate that as a priority on your matrix.

This becomes the tool for recruiting new board members – a strategic process that is related to the institutional plan and will ensure a board that supports organizational development.

Develop and implement a board recruitment policy and process.

Once the matrix is in place, there needs to be a process to support the matrix.

Discourage, but don't eliminate, "opportunistic" recruits. These are people who may not fall into a matrix cell, but who have such interest, passion, or potential that they should be asked to join the board.

Some of these may be "new philanthropist" investors who

want to be on the board because they feel like they are significant stakeholders (see chapter on "Transformational Gifts").

With a few exceptions, the remainder of the recruitment should be done according to an approved process and within any policies you may wish to develop. Be sure all board members, but especially the Board Development Committee, have a copy of the process, the policy, and the matrix.

Dissolve the Nominating Committee and replace it with a Board Development Committee (or a Committee on Directors or a Committee on Trustees).

A Board Development Committee has a much larger mandate than merely nominating new board members. It is responsible for recruiting, cultivating, enlisting, monitoring, encouraging, orienting, and (heaven forbid!) de-enlisting if board members don't meet the basic requirements of board membership.

This committee develops the board member handbook, conducts the orientation, and is committed to keeping a "stable" of ready recruits at all times.

Unlike a Nominating Committee, which meets just before the slate of candidates is due, the Board Development Committee meets at least quarterly, reviewing prospects, cultivating them, and bringing names and profiles to the board for its review all year round.

Prepare and approve a board member job description.

Specifically, be certain to state expectations regarding financial support, attendance at meetings, committee membership, attendance at events, fiscal and legal responsibility, evaluation of executive director, and other related functions.

In addition, add some expectations that are more attitudinal than performance-based: loyalty in time of crisis, willingness to communicate concerns through appropriate channels, respect for staff, and willingness to use appropriate channels for approaching staff. Unless stated, these can become difficult issues in times of crisis or transition.

Do "prospecting" for board members, using the board matrix.

Just as you gather names of prospective donors from board members and the community, you should also do the same for generating names of potential board members. Many boards do this, but it is a random process. Systematize it.

Have board members bring at least one name in at each board meeting. Have senior staff members do the same. Once you have given the Board Development Committee the names, they should use the same process as is used for developing fund raising prospect lists: qualify the names by contacting the individual who suggested the name, getting as much information as possible; developing a strategy for recruitment; cultivating the prospective board member with lunch meetings, tours, visits to board meetings and other opportunities to meet people and learn more about the organization.

There may be some potential candidates who want to serve on committees. This is a great proving ground, and provides both candidate and organization an opportunity to see if there is a fit.

At a certain point in the developing relationship, you'll know if this is a potential board member. If there is a good match, and if there's an appropriate opening, you can enlist. If there's not an opening, you'll need to keep the candidate involved and interested until such time.

In your recruitment and enlistment, don't focus only on the

expertise (banking, legal, fundraising, marketing) that the new board member will bring to the organization.

Focus also on the mission, vision, passion, and values of the organization. In this way, you will avoid having board members who lack this necessary passion to make balanced decisions.

Your goal is to have passionate pragmatists on your board. Without passion, advocacy is often minimal. Remember that there are two bottom lines for nonprofits: the values return, and the financial stability. Passionate pragmatists understand both.

A board that thrives and serves the organization well is one that is truly involved.

Once you have recruited and enlisted new board members, using a process and matrix that indicates that you're serious about board member service, don't let the board member down by failing to involve him.

Active involvement in committees and activities is an obvious responsibility, but there's also the involvement in decision-making and policy-making.

Sometimes very strong executive directors with strong executive committees want to make all the decisions and create all the policies, using the board as a rubber stamp. This is the quickest route to losing good board members.

On one board, an individual with a great deal to offer became so frustrated that she resigned after three meetings. Basically, she reported there was nothing to do. Everything was predetermined before the meeting. Although involved on a committee, it wasn't enough. She wanted to be involved in discussions and decisions around issues.

Board meetings must be relevant, interesting, marked by

dialogue and discussion, and should never be a waste of time.

Publish a board calendar at the beginning of the year. Make sure the board meeting dates are easy to track (2nd Tuesday of every other month) and that the calendar is adhered to except in emergencies.

Construct agenda that include a "mission message" (a testimonial or presentation by a client or constituent or member of the community who has benefited from your work in the middle of the session). Devote time at each meeting to an issue of importance, not just to committee reports and other predictable agenda items. Promote dialogue and discussion. Control those who would dominate by having strong board leadership chair the meeting.

Celebrate your board and let them get to know each other (if they choose) outside of board meetings.

Those who come together to decide the future and fate of our nonprofits have agreed to a very important responsibility. The meetings, while enjoyable, have a serious purpose. Injecting warmth and humor into the board meetings can go a long way.

Have an annual retreat, where there's time for casual interaction and even some planned activities to enhance knowledge of each other. Give an award to board members that has a bit of whimsy attached.

One board, which had undergone a considerable growth transition (from five to 15 members) and was trying diligently to become more committed, dreamed up a great award. They were discussing the difference between involvement and commitment, and were told by a facilitator that the difference was best illustrated by consideration of a breakfast of ham and eggs.

In that breakfast, they were told, the chicken was involved, but the pig was committed. The board members decided to give the "pig award" at each meeting to the board member who had shown the most commitment. And so it began: a Miss Piggy magnet circulated from refrigerators to filing cabinets for years, reminding each meeting's winner that others were grateful for their commitment.

Social events for board members (dinners, picnics) can also be held, but remember that not all board members will want to participate. The purpose is to bring board members closer together so they will understand the texture and dynamics of themselves as a board and will be able to reach decisions and grapple with issues more effectively.

•••

Board members are an organization's major investors, regardless of the size of the gift they make. The time, effort and advocacy they give, in addition to their gifts, have a huge impact on the overall health and community perception of the organization. When recruited and enlisted appropriately, and involved and engaged during their board service, they will thrive. And so will your organization.

23

THE DYNAMICS OF SUCCESSFUL BOARD MEETINGS

Do your board members look forward to board meetings? No, I'm not joking. There are actually organizations where board members *like* attending board meetings. They find them stimulating, interesting, informative, and motivating.

But sadly, this seems to be the exception.

More common is the experience of a high-profile, much-sought-after board member who resigned after his first meeting. He specifically cited the dynamics of the board meeting as the reason for his departure. It was, in his words, "just not for him."

Another individual, a busy entrepreneur, recently said he'd never join another board because it was only about talk, talk, talk. No action. And, therefore, not his "cup of tea."

Across all kinds of organizations, the attitude of board members towards attending board meetings runs on a scale from *dread* to *avoid* to *endure* to *duty* to *enjoyment*. Where would your organization fit on this scale?

If you want to have board members look forward to meetings, here's what you should know about the dynamics of successful meetings.

That may sound obvious, but beyond talk, too little is accomplished at many board meetings. To stay energized, people need a sense of completion and closure on important items.

If you don't have a quorum, no decisions can be made. Worse, even with a quorum, there may not *be* decisions to make. Why come to a board meeting, then?

Be sure you have action items on your agenda and that they are acted on. And, be sure you report on the results of actions board members have taken previously.

People are heard.

If the *real* board meeting is taking place in the parking lot or on cell phones *after* the meeting, then you should look into the way discussion is handled during the meeting.

Are there a few who dominate to the exclusion of others? Are new ideas welcome, or are they dismissed with the tired bromide, "We tried that once and it didn't work"?

If people have issues, is there a process to ensure that the issue gets on the board agenda and a well-facilitated discussion to see that the issue is heard?

When people can participate fully at a meeting, their engagement increases. When they're ignored or shut down, they detach from the meeting and, in many cases, from the organization.

The meeting is well-run.

Does your chair know how to run a meeting, or does she need some coaching?

While you shouldn't choose a board chair only because she can run a meeting, it is something to consider. And, if she's qualified in every other way, but the meetings are drifting, off task, and dull, then her leadership won't have the desired impact.

Most communities have management support organizations that coach people in running better meetings. It would be worth the investment to send not only your chair, but all committee chairs as well.

There is a generous exposure to mission, not just administrative concerns.

Every board meeting should have a "mission moment" – a five-minute session in the middle of the meeting where you hear from a client, grateful patient, music student, alum, parent, or whoever can speak with passion about the impact of your organization in their lives.

Do this in the middle of the meeting to catch the latecomers and the early-leavers.

Reports by program staff don't carry the same passion and authenticity. You need to hear it from the source.

There are opportunities for site visits.

Whatever your service, think of ways to get your board members into the place where the work happens — at least once a year.

If your organization's work isn't something outsiders can observe (mental health, prison work, medical programs with at-risk patients), then take board members to the site and have a presentation from physicians or other relevant experts about the latest breakthroughs in research, treatment, or care.

Let them see the facility and meet the staff, even if they can't watch the work. Board members connect in new ways when they have this experience.

Board members have fun, and there is an appreciation of good humor.

Our work is serious, but that doesn't mean board meetings can't be fun. Encourage humor and interaction. Laughter is a great catalyst for deepening engagement.

Shared humor creates closer ties among the board members, creating a stronger sense of team. Board meeting dynamics that are relaxed, warm, and accepting have a powerful effect on members, diminishing their sense of reserve and allowing their humor and ease of expression to emerge.

Moreover, you don't have to abandon rules and structure to create such an environment.

Successes are shared.

Starting the meeting with an SOS (Share Our Success) session is a great way to get people thinking about their interaction with the organization.

At first, the board chair will probably have to ask some members before the meeting to share a story of a solicitation, a meeting, a random conversation in which there was, for example, unsolicited praise for the organization.

After a few meetings, once board members see this as a constructive measure, setting the tone for positive interaction, the challenge will be to keep the SOS stories to a limit.

Meeting logistics are clear and observed.

Start on time.

Keep the agenda moving (a timed agenda works for some organizations — each item is limited so everything can be covered).

And if the usual length of the meeting has to be expanded because of a serious item of business, let people know in advance and discuss the extension at the beginning of the board meeting.

The boardroom environment is conducive to doing business.

Except for the site-based meeting, board meetings should be held in the organization's boardroom if there is one, or in another facility with a board meeting area that's conducive to maintaining a professional image.

Gone are the days when organizations needed to look poor to raise money. Now, we realize that the confidence people place in an organization is the basis of their investment.

Their confidence is lessened when they're brought to a shabby room with mismatched chairs, worn carpet, peeling paint, and other indications of deferred maintenance.

They understand that their job is governance, not management.

This distinction makes all the difference in the dynamics of board meetings.

It keeps board members at the right level of discussion, and (hopefully) prevents them from sinking into the mire of management issues belonging to the staff. The focus on governance is established through the agenda and the items emphasized.

It is also a result of keeping the detail work – including work with the staff on operational issues – in committees and letting the outcomes and recommendations of those meetings be reported as a framework for making quality governance decisions –decisions on policies, strategies, and evaluation.

•••

Effective board meeting dynamics are a surprisingly important point for overall board member satisfaction. Good board meetings energize, motivate, inform, inspire, satisfy, and renew enthusiasm for service to the organization.

If attendance at your board meetings has declined, evaluate

the quality and dynamics of your board meetings. Maybe people have checked out because the meetings were so deadly dull, contentious, or meaningless. Fortunately, with the above suggestions in mind, this problem is relatively easy to remedy.

24

RECRUITING YOUNGER PEOPLE FOR YOUR BOARD

Let's face it. None of us is getting any younger. And, when you look around the boardroom table, that fact becomes alarmingly apparent.

When we consider the number of younger people – those in their 20s, 30s and 40s – who stepped forward as volunteers or donor-investors during the roaring economy of 1990s, we should now see a proportionate number involved as board members or as committee or task force members. We should, but we don't. These younger investors aren't involved in any great numbers with governance, policy, and planning.

We know we need young people to infuse our organizations with ideas, energy, and a new generation of connections and commitment. As a result, the recruitment matrix for most nonprofit boards calls for diversity of race, ethnicity, geography, skills, interests, expertise, and age. But, of all of those vectors, the one still ignored in most recruitment is age.

The dilemma has two dimensions. In perpetuating their boards, board members seek those like themselves — in general, people in their 50s, 60s and 70s. Some board members, as well, say they don't know where to look for younger members. This is no excuse. However, there is another reason why younger people are not on boards in the numbers they should be.

When observing or interacting with boards at events or occasional meetings, younger people often don't like what they see -- namely "bored" meetings in which politics and power issues, endless discussions, absence of mission message, and a focus on "administrivia" lead them to feel negatively about board service.

How can we successfully recruit younger people to our boards? First, by opening our minds and eyes to the talents they bring and then by reaching out in entirely new recruitment arenas and engaging them.

But second, by ensuring that what they would find when joining your board is what they're looking for. The environment you create and the image you project will have a great deal to do with your successful recruitment, enlistment, and retention of the next generation of leaders.

Here's what you should know about what younger people are looking for in an organization.

Focus.

Youth has always been impatient, but this is a more impatient generation than most boards are used to. As a result, it's very important to stay focused yet responsive in board meeting discussions.

Run your board meetings well. Have a mission and vision that are evident, and tasks supporting them that are well organized, assigned, and evaluated.

Confine board discussions to the key points that need to be reviewed in order to make a decision – leave deeper explorations of issues and nuances to committee meetings and bring the essence to the board.

Otherwise, you'll lose the attention and interest of this

younger generation who may process things more quickly or bring a different style of analysis to the table.

Relevance.

This is key. Your organization's mission – as the expression of why you exist – must be relevant to the community needs you're meeting. Derived from that, your programs and actions must be relevant, too.

There are plenty of problems and lots of opportunities in society – particularly now – and it's important not to waste people's time with irrelevant issues.

Continually assess your relevance by looking into the community for trends and needs. Transparency is a key value among newer investors of all ages. Evaluate not only your programs but also the relevancy of your board's work and honestly report your findings.

Action.

Nonprofits are change agents and yet we're often reluctant to change. We hide behind dialogue and deliberation and sometimes delay implementation beyond the tolerance of our donors or the needs of the community.

Younger people are looking for action, not talk. Many feel we have talked some issues into inertia without solving them (in some communities, homelessness is a major example). They seek participation in actions to correct, address, or solve the problems that have been around for their entire lives. In short, they want to get on with it.

Impact.

Younger people are looking for measurable impact of their

financial and time involvement. They want to know how many people you're serving, how many are attending the concert, or how many signed up for the run. Then, they want to know how much money you raised, how it will be spent, and what difference will be made by that investment.

Tell them the statistics, but enlarge their understanding of the sector by telling them stories, too. Let them meet people who have benefited from their investment. Engage them in backstage or behind the scenes opportunities with performing and visual arts – and let them see, as well, the impact you are having on school children, seniors, or others you serve.

Having program staff describe the impact isn't good enough – you need to let board members (of all ages) see it, hear it, and know it from those who have directly or indirectly benefited from your work.

Involvement.

The desire of younger investors to be involved with the programs in which they have invested is keen.

Young people, working together in local organizations, have for several generations made an impact on our communities. They volunteer in hospitals, in summer camps, with seniors and the disabled, and behind the scenes in the performing and visual arts.

Why should they have to stop this direct involvement when they reach the age and station in life when they're considered for board service? Sitting at a boardroom table once a month (or six times a year or once a quarter) cannot and should not substitute for hands-on experience with the programs themselves.

Don't lose sight of this – younger people want this (and, by the way, older board members benefit from this kind of involvement, too!).

Connections.

One reason younger people come on the board is the same reason older people do: to be with others who share their values and interests. But with younger people there's an added reason – they can operate as peers (on the board) with people who by reason of profession or reputation are vastly senior to them.

This is a wonderful opportunity to work with and observe people who become role models for them in both their board work and their professional lives. It is a true "perk" that becomes very appealing to younger people in the recruitment process.

And, on the other side of the equation, younger people bring new connections to your organization – ones that will still be active when you've decided to retire from active service.

Fun.

Let's not forget this. Younger people really want to have fun when they give their time to an organization or cause. Be sure your board knows how to have fun – not just at parties, but at the board meetings as well. A humorless board meeting is a terrible experience for anyone.

Admittedly, if the business of the meeting is grim or very serious, you cannot focus on fun. But, for the most part, we take board business entirely too seriously – failing to see that even if our work is serious (which it is) we don't need to ban laughter or lightness or fun from the boardroom.

Many a difficult issue has been resolved when someone had the courage to see the humor, irony, or absurdity of the situation.

Growth.

The opportunity to work with those who are senior to them in age and accomplishment is a tremendous source of growth for many younger people.

When setting up "buddies" or mentors on the board to help them get acquainted with the people and the system, link younger board members with more senior ones from whom they can learn not only about your organization, but about skills or professions that may be similar to their ambitions.

In your formation of committees or task forces, find out from these younger members what skills they bring and what they would like to learn.

Finally, in your board meetings, follow procedures and practices that give younger board members a solid foundation in what you hope will be a lifetime of service to the nonprofit sector.

Leverage.

Let younger people see that their board service can be leverage in their lives. While the time they spend with your organization will detract from the time they may have for other pursuits, they should realize that this experience gives them a new circle of people with whom to build relationships now and in the future.

Their role in fundraising and other community outreach will provide connections and visibility that can be an enhancement to their own personal goals. And, the connections they bring – with the next generation – can only better leverage the future of the organization.

Skills.

People of all ages bring skills and learn skills when they're on a board. It's too easy to think that younger people stand more to gain than give when they come on our boards. Get rid of that idea.

Young people bring ease with technology, agility at problem solving, understanding about what marketing works with their own age group, innovative approaches to problems that have challenged us older folks for years, and other skills that we must fathom and savor and appreciate.

We can learn much from them, and they from us. Having younger people on board can result in mutual skill sharpening and sharing.

•••

Reducing the average age of your board by getting younger people on it is a worthy idea. If you've hesitated to expand your matrix, or haven't assessed how appealing your board would be to younger members, now is the time.

Begin thinking about the sons and daughters of those people you have served on boards with, and also about those young people known to those sons and daughters, who are new to the community, vitally interested in becoming active, and who would welcome the many opportunities board service can provide.

And, in the process, you will find a refreshing source of new ideas, abundant energy, fresh perspective and new linkages. And, guess what: you will find the older folks are energized too.

25

KEEPING YOUR BOARD AND STAFF PARTNERSHIP IN BALANCE

Balance is often an elusive state. We seek it in our lives and in our organizations. In mission-based community nonprofits, the balance in board-staff roles often determines a healthy organization.

Those organizations in which board and staff understand their individual roles, and support one another, are uniquely equipped for success. When organizations are out of balance and tensions arise over respective roles, the conflict can blur the focus on mission and diminish the capacity to succeed.

The nonprofit sector is built on partnerships. We're partners with the community in solving problems and enhancing the quality of life. We initiate partnerships with funders for the mutual accomplishment of our mission, and with volunteers to help us leverage time and money in the most effective way possible. The dual leadership structure of nonprofits, in which board and staff share responsibility for the organization, is itself a preeminent nonprofit partnership.

Maintaining a balanced environment in which partnerships flourish can be challenging. But it is worth the effort. Here's what you should know about keeping your board-staff partnership in balance.

Be sure board and staff have a shared vision and that they understand how that vision will be achieved.

Don't assume people are on the same page relative to the vision. If it has been a while since your organization voiced its vision, make that a top priority for your next board-staff retreat. The heart of all successful partnerships, and the fulcrum for maintaining balance, is a shared vision.

When board and staff members come together to create and commit to a shared vision, they are energized around their areas of common agreement. It then becomes easier to delineate the roles of board and staff in working towards that vision.

Be sure both board and staff are involved in strategic planning.

Whatever planning approach you use (board driven or staff driven), be sure both board and staff are full participants in the process and in the ultimate ownership of the plan. Nothing throws a board-staff partnership off balance more dramatically than plans generated by either board or staff without adequate input from the other.

If you do your planning at an annual retreat, make sure it is a *board-staff* retreat. Excluding one of the partners is the best way to kill a partnership. Exclusion builds suspicion and mistrust and leads to "border crossing," that is, the tendency of boards and staffs to cross into each other's territory because they feel shut off from the vision and the process of setting goals and objectives. This applies to budgeting as well, the "price tag" for the plan. Budgeting must be an inclusive process in which there's both board and staff involvement, input, review, and approval.

Define board and staff roles clearly and often.

All staff members should have written job descriptions. So should all volunteers, including board members. When provided with a written job description, board members view their responsibilities more seriously.

In addition to their own job descriptions, provide board members with the job descriptions of the key individuals with whom they'll be working (administrative, development, and program staff leaders). Give them job descriptions for the committees to which they've been assigned.

With this information in hand, board members get a better idea of their role and a greater sense of being a partner with staff in the mutual achievement of the organization's mission.

Set mutual expectations and evaluate often.

In addition to job descriptions, which outline individual and committee responsibilities, it's a good idea to annually share expectations among board and staff leadership. Daily, we evaluate people on our expectations of them. But too often, they don't know what those expectations are. Expectations and responsibilities are linked, but different.

A board member's responsibility may be to attend board meetings regularly. But, the expectation of the executive director may be that board materials will have been read and that meetings will start on time. Irritation can lead to strife.

An annual setting of expectations is a good idea. And, facilitated well, this session needn't be dreaded. It's merely a chance to let the board say to staff what their expectations are, and for staff to relay theirs to the board.

Evaluation of volunteers and an annual board self-evaluation also keep the partnership strong and in balance.

Revisit the mission at every opportunity.

The mission is why you exist as an organization. It is the community need you are meeting. It is the glue binding board and staff members together. It is the inspiration for dealing with the mundane and for stretching to do the exceptional. To revisit it isn't to re-read a statement: it is to witness first hand the impact of your organization's work in the community.

It's easy for staff and board to become so consumed with service delivery or with generating the resources that they fail to see the impact of what they're doing. You'll create stronger partnerships and keep the momentum brisk by continually presenting to both board and staff the intertwined nature of what each does: the board generates financial and human resources, which provide staff with what they need to do their job, which in turn has an impact on the community.

Keep both board and staff connected with that impact. Invite those who have benefited to tell their stories. This kind of "product demonstration" is a tremendously effective way to keep the sense of partnership and maintain balance. Each person feels as though his or her role is important because the results are so apparent.

Create an environment of mutual respect.

If an organization doesn't really respect volunteer input and involvement, it will show. No amount of lip service will mask the lack of basic commitment to the importance of board-staff partnerships. Volunteers know when they are tolerated, not really accepted.

Because volunteer involvement is mandated in our sector (hence, the term "voluntary sector"), the absence of visible commitment to a true partnership is sometimes an invitation for boards to circle the wagons and become a divisive force. They step into areas where staff does not want them, principally because they've been denied a role and place in the areas where they could be effective.

Mutual respect is created (or recreated) when this issue is dealt with, when board-staff roles are clearly defined, and when appropriate avenues for board (and other volunteer) involvement are delineated.

Watch for symptoms of mission drift.

Mission drift is serious. It's a result of an erosion of the board-staff partnership. Its symptoms are those of an organization out of balance. The symptoms are:

• Board meetings in which there's little or no mention of the programs or services except in the financial report.

• Board members who refuse to get involved with the organization except at board meetings and make little or no financial commitment.

• Leaders who fail to encourage leadership growth and succession.

• Battles for control between board and staff.

• An approach to organizational priorities that ignores the needs of constituencies and changes in the marketplace.

• A shift from the passionate commitment that characterizes board membership in an organization in its early stages to an overly pragmatic view often found among board members in organizations with greater maturity.

Reward teamwork.

It is important to reward and recognize individual achievements among board and staff members who fulfill their roles well, but it's equally important to verbally and visibly reward teamwork. When projects, programs, or events are the result of effective partnerships working in balance, let that be known. Cite the efforts that were made to include staff and volunteers, and emphasize the way in which each fulfilled their defined roles.

Make sure the reward and recognition you offer is framed by the shared vision and the way in which the achievement or event supports that vision. Stress the impact it will have on the organization and the community.

View each opportunity for reward or recognition as a way to strengthen partnerships and increase balance.

Set standards and adhere to them.

Most people who become involved as staff and board leaders want standards. They want accountability. They want to be evaluated. They are inspired by a commitment to quality and excellence, and will advance that commitment through their own work if the standards are set.

Often, we erode the partnership balance by not setting standards. If your organization is important to the community, then the work of staff and volunteers must be of the best quality. Convey that. It will instill a culture of pride and help ensure the highest performance by everyone.

Communicate openly and often regarding progress, challenges and opportunities.

Partnerships and balance are eroded when either board or staff feels they are kept in the dark about policies, operations, crises, opportunities, or other issues. Establish regular communication avenues between board and staff and guard against an "us and them" organizational culture. The more personal the communication, the more effective. While e-mail is efficient, it lacks warmth and should be balanced with verbal or written communication.

Engage board and staff in ad hoc opportunities to address opportunities or challenges that arise between formal meetings. Brown bag discussion sessions and other informal opportunities increase the sense of trust and partnership. Invite staff and board to casual meetings to meet a visiting professional or to discuss a pertinent issue in the community that could have an impact on program or services. Circulate "draft" documents for board comment.

Good communication is a major factor in maintaining both effective partnerships between board and staff and the appropriate balance in roles.

•••

Investing in strategies to keep board-staff roles balanced, and to keep partnerships strong, is a critical function of healthy nonprofits. These suggestions should help your organization maintain balanced relationships and a focus on mission.

26

ORGANIZING A SUCCESSFUL BOARD RETREAT

Whether your organization already has a tradition of an annual board retreat, or is considering one for the first time, there are a host of approaches and practices that will help your next retreat be more productive, relevant, and enjoyable.

Often based around institutional or development planning and evaluation, and frequently held at a site away from the organization's usual meeting facility, retreats offer a unique opportunity for board and staff members to get to know each other and the organization better. Because retreats are longer than regular board meetings, there is time to focus on mission, vision, values, and issues, rather than just on reports and action items.

A successful board retreat can be a catalyst for change and innovation; a failed retreat can be a disastrous setback. Here's what you should know about organizing a successful board retreat.

You may have to do a selling job to get your board members to buy-in.

If it's the first time you've attempted to organize a board retreat -- or if previous retreats have been viewed as a waste --

there may be mild to severe resistance from the board. This is especially true if board commitment is uneven and leadership is skeptical of the importance of an extended session. Convincing boards it's vital for them to spend four hours (the minimum time for a "retreat") to three days (probably the maximum time) may be difficult.

Choose a date, place, length of session, and format that are both acceptable and appealing. Encourage discussion of the retreat idea at a board meeting, and gain the broadest possible consensus. Then, develop a solid outcomes-focused agenda to lure these committed but very busy people, and send out a notice stating:

• Why the retreat is important at this time (for example, a change in the funding base, need to evaluate the market for services, potential for new funding),

• What the principal goals are (for example, setting the groundwork for a new long-range plan or a development plan of action),

• The process that will be used to achieve the goals (presentations, facilitated discussions, small group meetings), and

• Why board participation is key to the retreat's success.

At a board and/or staff meeting three to four months prior to the retreat, determine the length of the retreat (based on the tolerance of the participants and the need to spend time together to address and resolve issues). It's best to start with a short good retreat and gradually, over the years, extend the time as the need demands.

Be inclusive, not exclusive, when developing the list of who will attend, and make sure to include all those whose presence is needed to ensure the desired outcomes.

In addition to members of the board, include key administrative, development, and program staff at your retreat to ensure clarity and continuity in fulfilling plans that are devised at the retreat. Small organizations in which there may be much shared responsibility between board and staff often include the entire staff at the retreat. Failure to include any staff except the executive director can lead to feelings of "us versus them."

There are exceptions, of course. Some board retreats are called for the express purpose of addressing crucial staffing issues which may involve the executive director. In these cases, the retreat usually begins with an executive session where only board members are in attendance. When their business is finished, the executive director or other involved staff members are invited to join and to discuss the results of the board deliberations and to begin working towards implementation of changes that must be made. Needless to say, these latter kinds of retreats are tough, tense meetings.

Fortunately, the vast majority of board retreats aren't grim gatherings at which sensitive personnel issues are resolved. Most are great opportunities for exploring issues and ideas in a more relaxed environment and for spending time getting to know each other.

Enlist a retreat planning committee whose members are representative of those who will attend.

Committee members become the principal advocates for the retreat, so they must represent both board and staff if both will be included at the retreat. They need to be clear and consistent in conveying the importance of the meeting and the anticipated outcomes to others. Give the committee chair time on board and staff agendas during the ramp-up period to the retreat: encourage a bit of cheerleading to keep interest and attendance up.

Allow ample time for the planning committee to develop the agenda, make the arrangements, organize the program to ensure the outcomes, and build in activities to help people get to know each other better.

Planning should begin three to four months before the retreat. If you do an annual retreat, it should be done the same month each year, and be built into the regular board meeting calendar. In this way, you're more likely to have a date that's convenient for most of the board members.

The committee should establish preliminary desired outcomes (both results and process outcomes) and submit a tentative agenda to the board for feedback at least three months before the anticipated retreat. Include the facilitator (see below) in the planning meetings to the extent possible. She needs to understand the dynamics and the issues. Provide the facilitator with a list of the outcomes you want (she may want to prepare the initial agenda).

Supply the committee with notes and minutes from past retreats. If this is your first retreat, it's helpful for someone from the committee to be connected with a board or staff member from another organization that is experienced with board retreats. Much can be learned from such an exchange, and the knowledge can make the difference between an average and an outstanding first retreat.

Be sure the agenda mixes information, inspiration, and motivation.

These are three frames for organizing a retreat: they are also three important outcomes. *Inspiration* is provided by bringing the "product" to the retreat. One retreat succeeded in persuading reluctant board members to become active in a stalled capital campaign by bringing in three recipients of grants from the fund the organization was trying to expand. Each person spoke of the impact the scholarships had made on their lives, and thanked the board and staff members for making it possible for them to achieve their personal and professional goals.

Information is also a critical ingredient. Be sure the facts are current, accurate, and presented in a form which stimulates discussion and can be used by board and staff members as they connect with others in the community.

Motivation is, like the others, both an ingredient and an outcome. People are motivated to be advocates for an organization when there is a feeling of confidence that their efforts will be valued, appreciated, and make a difference. This part of the retreat is locked in when program or administrative staff convey to the development staff and the board members how critical their efforts are to the capacity of the organization to meet community needs.

Motivation is also stimulated by having each retreat participant, at the end of the session, tell the others what their commitment is to see that the outcomes of the retreat are implemented. Note is made of each commitment, and the thank you letter to each participant includes that individual's specific commitment.

Seek 100 percent attendance; be happy with 85 percent; cancel if only 70 percent sign up.

It simply is not worth the effort and cost (place, facilitator, refreshments) if too few people participate. Early notice of the date, consideration of people's tolerance regarding the length of the meeting, the distance they may have to travel to get there, and other factors can also improve attendance.

Use a call-down process by committee members to reconfirm

attendance two weeks to 10 days before the retreat. If there's dramatic fall-off in attendance, have the board chair or executive director call each board person. If that does not work, consider cancellation.

Decide early in your planning if you'll use an inside or outside facilitator.

Inside facilitators come without cost, but may lack the required objectivity. The advantage of an outside facilitator is professional skill and the objectivity to move the meeting along and not get tangled up in politics or difficult relationships. The principal disadvantage is cost ($500 to $3000 or more a day).

In some communities, local foundations will cover the cost of a facilitator if the retreat objectives are clearly tied to, for example, long range planning.

If you choose to use an outside facilitator, check with others who have used the person to verify effectiveness and appropriateness for your retreat. Also, be sure she's available before you confirm the date with the participants and the facility.

Moreover, it's a good idea to have a backup facilitator in mind just in case the date doesn't work. Involve the facilitator in the retreat planning: do not bring a facilitator in cold to a retreat.

Disarm all potentially explosive individuals and issues before the retreat or, if that's not possible, be sure the facilitator and participants are aware the situation may be volatile.

Potentially explosive individuals or issues may find their way into the retreat. These land mines have exploded the agenda of more than one well-planned retreat. When the facilitator, committee, and participants are aware of the danger spots and of people who may have volatility around certain issues, there is opportunity to be sensitive to the issues and individuals and hopefully use the retreat as a forum for building consensus and shared vision.

A skillful facilitator can sometimes bring these issues to the surface within the context of a larger discussion and in such a way that they are addressed objectively. This can help neutralize the tension so issues can be dealt with openly and individuals with concerns about these issues feel respected and heard.

As the retreat approaches, keep the reminders and the information flowing.

At the retreat, stay on time and on point to the extent possible and troubleshoot issues that could get in the way of the agenda. One week before the retreat, send out a final package with directions to the site (both map and narrative), advice about dress, information about the facility (bring your swim suit or tennis racket), final agenda/schedule, and any last minute background reading materials or other information needed to enhance the agenda.

At the retreat, be diligent about starting and ending sessions on time, and keeping the sessions lively. Handle disruptive people or difficult issues with skill and tact.

Small group sessions are excellent for team building, and for allowing people to relax and have fun. Be sure each session within the retreat has value and connection to the outcomes of the retreat: people resent spending time on unrelated activities when they feel they should be pursuing the agenda. Save the "unrelated" activities for lunch, breaks, or sports activities conducted after the session or between sessions.

People quickly understand and appreciate a professionally-run meeting. Your board and staff members are key investors in the organization, and a well-run productive retreat is one way to honor their investment.

Have solid closure to the retreat.

In addition to the commitments from each participant, give participants a real sense of both the process and the product of the session. Much happens during a retreat, whether it's four hours or three days. Friendships are made. Tensions arise or are resolved. Plans are made or revised. Information is given and digested. There is time for reflection and comment.

Organizations miss an opportunity to further increase the impact of a retreat when they end the session in a haphazard way, with people drifting out with little understanding of the next steps or the purpose of their participation.

Allow enough time at the end of the retreat to do several things: a) confirm the next steps, including timeline, for any planning that has been done; b) make commitments; c) have the facilitator give her closing observations; and d) close with a short "stem winder" (inspirational talk) from a board member, staff leader, or the facilitator.

In the follow up letter to each participant, thank them for their contribution to the retreat and their commitment, summarize the outcomes of the session, recount some of the "process" moments that were fun and memorable, recap the next steps, and include complete notes from the retreat. This information should also be sent to those who could not attend the retreat, with a cover letter expressing the importance of the outcomes and the way they can participate now in the implementation of the decisions.

•••

Retreats that lack this thorough planning and follow-up may

be viewed by participants as isolated and time consuming experiences. By implementing these suggestions, you will be much more likely to have a successful retreat that will engage both board and staff while it is happening and ensure their continued commitment to its outcomes long after it is over.

27

COLLABORATING WITH OTHER ORGANIZATIONS

The squeeze in the nonprofit marketplace is being felt. Discerning donors are grappling with just where to put their money. In addition to looking at organizational performance, leadership, and impact, they're beginning to look for something else as well: evidence that the organizations they're funding are working together to deal effectively with common concerns and issues.

Multiple organizations that seem to be striving toward the same goal can be confusing to donors who are just looking for a way to make something happen. Often they can't tell the difference between the organizations and express wonder that there needs to be so many groups doing the same thing.

It would be a great boost for philanthropy if organizations could come together around common issues, develop a community marketing platform, and then provide an "investor's guide" to those interested in providing support. Instead, we're often so busy competing with one another we forget that our mission isn't what we are doing, it is *why* we are doing it and that what's important is the need we're *meeting*, not the need we *have* (for money).

Long ago, a colleague and I developed a campaign for two organizations that had decided to work together to raise awareness about domestic violence and collaborate in a community campaign (originally there were three organizations, but the third one withdrew because it didn't want to share its donor lists).

We had great public relations and marketing, and a successful community fund drive. But, at the end, quarreling arose over who should receive more of the money (despite our written agreement), with one organization claiming they had done more than the other. The effort was never repeated. A pity – because during that year the awareness about domestic violence significantly increased. The theme, "Breaking the Cycle of Violence" was compelling and the PSAs were around for years afterward.

If you too think working together is important, here is what you should know about exploring and creating opportunities for collaboration.

Engage the board in the vision and the potential impact of collaboration with other organizations.

Even if the idea for increased collaboration has come from the board, you still need to begin by working through all the benefits and pitfalls of the idea with the board. You can do this in broad strokes first and then, as you gather more information, bring back your data and present it.

Start by checking your by-laws and Articles of Incorporation to see if there's any prohibition against collaboration. If there is, you may want to initiate a revision process that can run in parallel with your fact finding so that you're ready if you decide to enter into partnerships with other organizations.

Once the board has given its approval to pursue the investigation and potential outreach to similar service providers, move forward with the following steps.

Analyze the market for services and the market for

fundraising.

At the outset, it is critical to know how aware people are of your mission and the community need you're addressing. Likewise, you need a grasp of the other organizations working in the same or similar areas.

Conduct a formal or informal market assessment of your visibility and perception. Then, work with your community foundation, professional association, or United Way to obtain a listing of similar service providers.

Find out as much as you can about these organizations – program delivery, fundraising, visibility and marketing – and develop a grid showing the organizations and the services they deliver, their budget, and the amount they raise. If you can also learn from what sources they raise their money, so much the better.

Chart the overlap of services, figure out the combined community investment in these programs, and then develop a brief report – including feedback from donor-investors wherever possible.

Convene a meeting of administrative leaders of similar service providers and review your findings.

Better yet, get some of them involved at the outset so they'll participate in the analysis. Review the findings. Share your grid. Gauge the response. See where there may be some initial opportunities for collaboration.

Capitalize on the areas of agreement, set some immediate goals, and enlist representatives of several organizations to work towards the implementation of these goals.

Introduce the idea of strategic collaboration with staff at each participating organization.

The idea of collaboration is a major shift for most organizations and needs to be accepted and embraced by program staff first, as they're usually the most affected.

When sharing your report, you will need to address the upside as well as the downside.

The upside is greater movement towards meeting the community needs to which you're dedicated – senior services, children's cultural programming, access for the disabled. For development staff, another upside is a wider marketing arena and the opportunity for significant investment in an issue, not just an organization.

The downsides are the impact of potential consolidation of programs or administrative functions across several organizations and the threat that poses to job security, as well as the reluctance of development staff to share lists if joint fundraising is planned.

In all likelihood, collaboration will *not* mean loss of jobs – it will mean an increase in the capacity to provide services.

Develop a marketing plan based on the issue you're addressing, and only secondarily on the organizations involved.

The domestic violence example in the introduction is a good one. The participating organizations (three, then two) met with a public relations and advertising firm that was willing to do a pro bono campaign.

The agency isolated the issue addressed by the women's shelter as well as the transitional housing program as "breaking the cycle of violence." All print and electronic messages were based on that theme. Stationery was created with that tagline and a listing of the two boards.

A domestic violence awareness day brought banners to the community's principal park, speeches by the County Supervisor and others, and great media coverage. The video PSAs were entirely focused on the issue of domestic violence, with only the closing cut line referring to the two participating agencies.

If you are going to do joint fundraising, get people from the various organizations involved.

Everything went well with the domestic violence fundraising collaboration cited above until it came time to divide the money.

The entire campaign was funded by a local foundation as part of a capacity building program (removing the risk factor for the organizations of trying something this bold).

Both boards and staffs participated in the development of the strategy for this annual campaign. They reviewed the fundraising materials (letters and brochures).

Each group even conducted some solicitation visits for leadership gifts.

While there were occasional hitches with this joint fundraising — especially when it came time to share lists — in the end more than $100,000 was raised and the visibility of the issue of domestic violence was significantly heightened.

Anticipate things that can go wrong with collaborations.

At the outset of the domestic violence program, an agreement was signed to divide the net proceeds equally. However, at the end, one organization felt it had contributed significantly more time to the effort and that more of its donors had participated. Consequently, the organization wanted a bigger piece of the pie.

As you would imagine, the collaboration suffered and the organizations ended the effort (even though the foundation that had funded them wanted the mutual effort to continue).

The biggest challenge to collaborations is overcoming the idea that combining efforts will diminish the perception or effectiveness of an organization. But in today's market, it can only *increase* the trust investors have in organizations to use their investment wisely. Make that point over and over.

Look at your work from the donor's perspective.

When issues of territory arise in the process of evaluating potential collaborations, step into the donor's shoes.

Let's say a donor cares about mental health. He is confronted with appeals from six organizations that somehow know he is interested in the issue. He wants to have an impact, but doesn't know which organization(s) to fund. If he gives to all six, it will dilute the impact of his gift. He feels frustrated.

Compare that to a donor who cares about mental health and receives a mailing that eloquently describes the need for effective mental health programs and services in her community. It lists the various organizations providing services and the people they serve.

She is then invited to make a larger investment in the overall work of these organizations – or to direct her gift to the one(s) working in the areas of greatest interest to her. The clarity gives her confidence about making an investment.

Which donor opportunity would you rather have?

Even if you have a unique market niche, there are still opportunities for collaboration.

If your services are very specialized, you may be thinking, "This doesn't apply to me." But, again, putting on the donor's shoes, think about your work relative to others' in this way.

Let's say your organization provides diagnostic and day treatment services for children with mental, emotional, neurological or educational disabilities. You are the only game in town.

However, there are donors who are concerned about these issues who are investing in a school for children with learning disabilities (many of whom you have probably diagnosed) or a residential treatment center for emotionally disabled young people (many of whom you may also have diagnosed).

One of the things that gives meaning to an investment is the notion that it has long term impact on a life or community. Work with organizations that represent a continuation or aspect of what you do. Present the idea of a continuum of services to the community, and how their investment in one or all of you provides a safety net for programs and lives.

Don't give up if the idea of collaboration doesn't take off immediately.

This is a tough proposition. It can be very threatening to an organization. Years ago, I conducted an audit of several environmental organizations working in the same community. They believed their work was sufficiently different that they resisted my recommendation of combining offices and administration and rallying the community around the larger issue of the environmental changes occurring then.

They dismissed my report and didn't hire me for further work, needless to say! About five years later, I received a call asking if I'd be interested in responding to an RFP to work with a new entity in this community – a collaborative of the five environmental organizations that I had recommended combining in my report.

It was a golden moment for me. The agencies were in the same office, sharing space, ideas, donor lists and marketing strategies and feeling as though their impact was greater than ever. The whole was, indeed, greater than the sum of its parts.

•••

The old ways are always easier. It's called the path of least resistance. But we are in a new marketplace dealing with increasingly discerning donors with fewer resources. They want to make the best investment.

Encourage their generosity through clarity. Eliminate confusion. A Roper Starch Worldwide poll in 2000 of Americans who *don't* give, found that more than half of the respondents (58 percent) said they had difficulty finding charitable groups that address causes important to them.

Donors are increasingly issues-focused and want to put their money where it will have the highest impact on the things they care about. We can help them by collaborating around our issues and mission. We need to get a message into the marketplace that tells them how their investment will have a greater impact than ever because we are partnering in new ways to maximize the difference they can make.

28

STRATEGIC INSTITUTIONAL PLANNING

To plan, or not to plan? Alas, that is no longer the question. The mandate is clear. Nonprofits are expected to have timely and relevant strategic plans.

Times have changed. Accountability and results are in; fuzziness and generalities are out.

While passion and faith still motivate our volunteers and donors, they like these feelings to be based in facts. They want to be reminded of the mission and vision and what we're doing to achieve both.

Prospective board members want to see the plan; potential investors want to know what will be done with their money.

Internally, the management team needs a roadmap. And the most useful tool for systematically accomplishing all of this is a solid strategic plan – one that involves both staff and board in the preparation, implementation, and evaluation process.

Here, then, is what you should know about the importance of strategic planning and how to engage board and staff members in the process.

Market the importance of planning to both board and staff.

There are those who believe that plans are worth little more than the paper they're written on. These are often the freewheeling, self-described highly creative people who feel that plans inhibit their freedom to innovate. In fact, most who use this excuse are really saying they don't want to be accountable. They don't understand that systems liberate.

Convincing these individuals to plan is a challenge. It may take time, or a crisis, or some straightforward internal marketing of two simple benefits of a well-formulated strategic plan:

• It conveys the vision, mission, and program goals that inspire people to give, join, and serve.

• With a solid financial plan attached, it is a critical internal tool for maintaining stability and strategic direction, and an important external tool for attracting funders and volunteers.

Learn to identify the sources of resistance to the idea of a strategic planning process, and prepare responses to those objections.

Both board and staff may resist planning for one or more of the following reasons:

• Answering pressing needs and problems takes precedence over the strategic planning process;

• Staff leadership is concerned about board member involvement in program planning and worried about issues of staff accountability;

• Board members are impatient with the planning process, feeling it requires a time-consuming analysis and discussion of issues they feel are obvious;

• Previous plans have gathered dust on the shelf and participants in earlier processes feel their efforts were wasted;

• The organization seems to be functioning well without one ("If it's not broken, why fix it?");

• There's a latent feeling by the board or staff leadership that the organization is so fragile that planning would be fruitless (as one board member remarked, "rather like rearranging deck chairs on the Titanic");

• The organization's board and staff leadership just don't know how to begin the process.

Finesse these objections as you talk to the board and staff, and find ways to address these points of resistance; otherwise, the plan will never happen.

With staff members, provide assurances that the board isn't taking over the management of the organization by getting involved in the strategic planning process.

This can be a tough hurdle in some organizations. Worried that board members may get too "hands on," staff may resist having board members get involved in planning.

Assure them that this is actually less apt to happen if the board is informed and involved in the planning process as well as the plan implementation. Board members who watch from the sidelines tend to get more easily angered or frustrated than those who are players in the game.

Let staff know that board-staff meetings during the planning process will promote greater understanding of the special role that each plays in the success of the organization. Provide staff with a clear picture of the role the planning task force and the entire board will play: lay out the steps from initial meeting through implementation and annual evaluation of the plan, and show how the partnership will work.

With board members, give them a clear definition of their role in the process, and how they will work in partnership with the staff.

Some board members will understand this right away; others may either be reluctant to get involved or eager to take over the process. Neither role benefits the process.

Form a board-staff planning task force, with a specific job description. When recruiting for this task force, let each member (board and staff) know why they've been selected and what expertise or perspective they bring (financial, legal, programmatic). Give them the planning schedule and deadlines, and provide samples of previous plans from your organization or other organizations.

One independent school, formulating its first comprehensive strategic plan (it had previously done curriculum plans) used its initial planning meeting as an opportunity to get acquainted with one another, the deadlines, and the process. There were parents, faculty, administrators, and parents of former students on the task force and after this "forming" meeting, they met frequently and productively to create a very strong plan.

Even if they understand their role, board members may still need to be convinced exactly why they need to spend their time in this process.

Try these arguments:

• The board is ultimately responsible for the mission and vision of the organization and the strategic planning process encourages careful evaluation of both;

• Boards are able to govern better when they understand the process and the assumptions behind the strategic plan;

• Because board members are removed from day-to-day operations of the organization, they bring a broader view and can be unencumbered change agents;

• As fundraisers, advocates, ambassadors, and coalition builders for the organization, board members must be involved in the planning process so they know what's going on with the organization;

• Board members provide the "window" into the community – they represent important constituencies and, without them, the planning process depends too heavily on "mirrors" for program and service evaluation;

• Board members' skills and experience add value to the planning process.

Use everyone's time wisely.

Planning can drag out. This is the surest way to lose both board and staff support for the process. Have a planning model that's easy to work with. You may have one you have used before, or one of your board members may have one.

Remember that all nonprofit activities really cluster in three areas:

Program (including facilities),

Organization (board and staff development) and,

Development (donor and fund development, marketing, public relations).

Years ago I began using these three areas as the template for the "Tri-POD" approach to planning. It has worked for many organizations.

Also, create a timeline and stick to it. Assign tasks and monitor their progress and completion. Work between meetings to refine and organize material generated at the meeting and circulate it to the members so that there's no "down time" at the next meeting.

Keep financial information flowing to test the appropriateness of goals and objectives – be sure the financial plan (two-year budget) is developed in parallel with the narrative plan.

Choose a leader, or co-leader, who is not only committed to the planning process, but who is strong enough to keep the process rolling.

Planning processes – and plans – thrive or fail based on the quality and determination of the leaders of the process. It also helps to have thick skin and broad shoulders.

Planning ignites passions and uncovers biases and emotions. Rejected ideas inflict untold hurts and frustrations, and long-held (but now perhaps irrelevant) dreams become insistent. The talent for listening, incorporating points of view, allowing the forum to unfold and for helping people feel valued (even when their ideas are rejected) is critical.

The leadership can come from the board or the staff, and co-chairs representing board and staff can work wonderfully. But, be sure that the individuals meet the criteria stated above. And, be certain your co-chairs share one vision. Otherwise, you may end up with conflict at the head of the table and dismay all around.

Communicate progress to those who are not involved on the task force.

Planning may be an alarming process for board and staff who aren't seated at the table. Devise ways to communicate during the process (email, newsletter, short summary letters) and, within defined limits, invite feedback at interim steps in the process.

Involve constituencies in "market" research to be sure their needs and ideas are reflected in the plan.

No strategic plan is complete without a framework of what the community thinks, wants, and needs. An independent school surveyed faculty, parents, parents of former students. A Boy Scout

Council conducted phone and in-person interviews with current and former leaders, past and present Scouts, as well as community leaders. A consortium of public school educational foundations surveyed its member districts and non-member districts.

The feedback from all of these surveys was used to validate existing goals and create new ones; it also provided valuable ideas for new strategies that addressed a changing marketplace.

Use the plan once it's done.

This may be the single biggest way to convey the importance of the process and the product, and the value of board and staff involvement. Don't let the plan gather dust. Use it. Challenge it. Revise it. Evaluate it honestly.

At every board meeting, see where you are with your plan. Link accomplishments to the power of having the plan. Tie fundraising successes to the importance of the plan to the donor. Annually, evaluate the year just past and add another year to the plan (this is called a "rolling base"). Every three years (or four or five) conduct another "zero based" process that takes everything down to root stock and gets people involved again in a major process like that described in this chapter.

•••

In today's demanding nonprofit world, we have no choice but to create strategic institutional plans. We must be entirely accountable, and willing to convey our impact and our results.

Development plans, once considered sufficient for fund raising purposes, have to be part of a larger architecture that encompasses board and staff development and program.

To be successful, planning must be viewed as important. To be accepted as important, planning must be successful. And, the success will depend on your ability to bring board and staff together in the process, and to listen to your community.

Companion Book to Fund Raising Realities

ASKING

A 59-Minute Guide to Everything Board Members, Volunteers, & Staff Must Know to Secure the Gift
by Jerold Panas, 112 pp. $24.95

It ranks right up there with public speaking. Nearly all of us fear it. And yet it is critical to our success.

Asking for money. It makes even the stout-hearted quiver.

But now comes a new book, *Asking: A 59-Minute Guide to Everything Board Members, Staff and Volunteers Must Know to Secure the Gift*. And short of a medical elixir, it's the next best thing for emboldening you, your board members and volunteers to ask with skill, finesse ... and powerful results.

Jerold Panas, who as a staff person, board member and volunteer has secured gifts ranging from $50 to $50 million, understands the art of asking perhaps better than anyone in America.

He knows what makes donors tick, he's intimately familiar with the anxieties of board members, and he fully understands the frustrations and exigencies of staff.

He has harnessed all of this knowledge and experience and produced what many are already calling a landmark book.

What *Asking* convincingly shows — and one reason staff will applaud the book and board members will devour it — is that it doesn't take stellar communication skills to be an effective asker.

Nearly everyone, regardless of their persuasive ability, can become an effective fundraiser if they follow a few step-by-step guidelines.

You have to know your cause, of course, and be committed to it. But, nearly as important, you have to know how to get the appointment, how to present your case, how to read your donor's words, how to handle objections, how to phrase your request, and even what behaviors to avoid.

Panas mines all of this territory, and because he speaks directly from his heart to the heart of board members, staff, and volunteers, the advice is authentic, credible, and ultimately inspiring.

INDEX

Angel, Karen, 47
American Fundraising
    Professionals (AFP), 187
Association of Healthcare
    Philanthropy (AHP), 187

Board development committee,
198-199
Boys and Girls Clubs, 123

Cal Tech, 123
Capacity-building grants, 127
Clark, Jim, 125
Coleman Institute, The, 123
College of the Ozarks, 123
Community Foundation Silicon
    Valley, 125, 126
Cornell University, 93
Corporate Cultures, 29
Council for Advancement and
    Support of Eduction (CASE),
    187
CUTCO cutlery, 96

Deal, Terrence E., 29

Djerassi Resident Artist Program, 41
Donor pyramid, 107
Drucker, Peter, 126
Dunlop, David, 93

El Pomar Foundation, 124
4-H Club, 131
Fund Raising School, The, 65
Future Shock, 161

George Washington University
    School of Medicine, 123
Glide Memorial Methodist
    Church, 169
Grace Episcopal Cathedral, 168

High Impact Philanthropy, 127

Iacocca, Lee, 30
Infoseek, 128
Intel, 123
Internet fundraising, 44-45

Job descriptions, 111, 176, 177

Kennedy, Allen F., 29

Kimball, Bill, 61
Kirsner, Scott, 128-129
Kirsch, Vanessa, 129

Levinson, Harry, 179
Line, Ray and Joanne, 126

Mission moment, 59, 205
Moore, Gordon, 123
Moves Management, 93
McKibben, Joe T.,

National Association of
    Independent Schools (NAIS),
    187
New Profit, 129
Nonprofit Motive, 128

Oakland Ballet, 42

Peters, Tom, 29, 35

Renewal Factor, The 35
Roper Starch Poll, 242
Rosso, Hank, 37, 65

Sage Hill School, 16, 125, 130
San Francisco Shakespeare
    Festival, 42
Seymour, Harold 'Sy', 37
SOS (Share Our Success), 206
Stanford, Jane, 52
Stanford University, 52, 61, 96,
    125, 130

Tauber, Laszlo, 123
Team solicitation, 87

UCLA, 125
University of Colorado, The, 123
University of Wisconsin, 125

Vector Health Programs, 47-48

Wall Street Journal, The, 126
Waterman, Bob, 29, 35
Wendroff, Alan, 127

Yale University School of
    Medicine, 50

LEARN MORE ABOUT FUNDRAISING AND NONPROFIT MANAGEMENT

If you want to hone your skills in fundraising, and stay abreast of developments in the field, subscribe to *Contributions* magazine, America's premier 'how-to' publication for nonprofit professionals.

Written by recognized authorities in the field, each issue contains in-depth information on:

- Raising major gifts
- Direct mail fundraising
- Planned giving
- Board development
- Public relations and marketing
- Nonprofit management
- Working with volunteers
- Using the Internet
- Grantseeking
- Donor research
- Developing leadership skills
- Corporate fundraising
- Trends in philanthropy
- Fundraising communications

To start your subscription ($40/year), call 508-359-0019 or visit www.contributionsmagazine.com.